T Dot Griots:

An Anthology of Toronto's Black Storytellers

Edited by
Steven Green and Karen Richardson

[signature: Karen L Richardson]

TRAFFORD

A cataloguing record for this book that includes the U.S. Library of Congress Classification number, the Library of Congress Call number and the Dewey Decimal cataloguing code is available from the National Library of Canada. The complete cataloguing record can be obtained from the National Library's online database at: www.nlc-bnc.ca/amicus/index-e.html
ISBN 1-55395-631-1

This book was published *on-demand* in cooperation with Trafford Publishing.
On-demand publishing is a unique process and service of making a book available for retail sale to the public taking advantage of on-demand manufacturing and Internet marketing. **On-demand publishing** includes promotions, retail sales, manufacturing, order fulfilment, accounting and collecting royalties on behalf of the author.

Suite 6E, 2333 Government St., Victoria, B.C. V8T 4P4, CANADA
Phone   250-383-6864   Toll-free   1-888-232-4444 (Canada & US)
Fax   250-383-6804   E-mail sales@trafford.com
Web site   www.trafford.com   TRAFFORD PUBLISHING IS A DIVISION OF TRAFFORD HOLDINGS LTD.
Trafford Catalogue #02-1347   www.trafford.com/robots/02-1347.html

10   9   8   7   6   5   4   3   2   1

Contents

Modern Griots, Ancient Roots

FOREWORD by DR. AFUA COOPER

This anthology resounds with the voices of poets, singers, storytellers and other word artists recounting their chronicles in multiple tones and registers. These raconteurs tell stories of anger and anguish, trials and tribulations, loss and lamentations, but also of pleasure and passion, redemption and revolution, love and liberty. Thus the voices are strong, probing, joyful, colourful, spectacular, spiritual, sombre but always hopeful. If there is a central theme that holds the anthology together it is that of redemption. Another thing. These lyric makers are all from Toronto and the GTA, thereby signalling to us that some of their stories come from concrete and glass skyscrapers, electric-songed streetcars and subway trains, and wide-lot housing developments with tree-lined streets in such places as Brampton. These narrators have come of age. They hold within themselves the multiple disguises of their city and these they want to reveal.

One might ask if there is a need for an anthology of contemporary Toronto storytellers and the answer is a resounding yes. In the past decade a new generation of urban griots have stormed the word scene bringing fresh voices and new agendas. Such names as Jason Kinte, nah-ee-lah/naila belvett, Kamau, Karen Richardson, Dwayne Morgan, Nana Yeboaa, d'bi.young, Motion, Travis Blackman, and a host of others, most of whom are represented in this collection, are putting their stamp on the spoken word movement in the GTA. Some of these artist-poets come from various spoken word traditions such as rap, dub poetry, literary recitations, sound poetry, nyahbinghi chants, or a mixture of two or more forms. Part of what makes this exciting is that these narrators are following in the footsteps of a long line of African spoken word artists.

In 1976, Harold Head, a South African poet living in exile in Toronto, edited the first Canadian anthology of black voices, *Canada in Us Now*, and heralded a movement of black arts anthologies from poetry to plays. Ann Wallace followed up in 1991 with *Daughters of the Sun, Women of the Moon*. Ayanna Black came on Wallace's heels in 1992 and 1994 with *Voices* and *Fiery Spirits* respectively. More followed. Makeda Silvera in 1993 with *The Other Woman*; and Djanet Sears with *Testifyin'* in 2000. Clearly, these numbers are too few given the plethora of black writers, poets, and storytellers in Canada. There has been an outpouring of magnificent literary work from black Canadians over the past thirty years, but the paucity of published works and CD productions would make one believe otherwise. That is why *T-Dot Griots* edited by Karen Richardson and Steven Green is so significant as it fills a wide gap in the African Canadian Arts movement, and it focuses on the new generation.

This collection, *T-Dot Griots*, celebrates bloodline and lineage by not only acknowledging the African culture of black Canadians, but also by linking us and our art to others who share our heritage and tradition across the globe. The editors have gone another step by naming these black Canadian wordsmiths, griots. This is a term used to describe the guardians and dispensers of the word in diverse

African cultures. For example, in the Manding culture of West Africa, the griot (the Manding word is *djeli*) was the historian, the bard, the moralist, and also an entertainer. The griot knew law, the griot knew tradition, the griot knew history, and s/he had the responsibility to pass these traditions on through words and performance to the rest of the community. The griot was also the conscience of the community. Royal courts had their own griots, individual monarch had her/his own griot who performed and spoke only for that particular monarch. Communities had their own griots, likewise countries and kingdoms. No community was complete without the griots for they were the ones who knew, they were the ones who had the responsibility to tell, instruct, and make whole. If there were no griots the body politic would fall apart because the griots were the ones who through their utterances and instructions, and the magic of their words provided the thread that kept the community together.

By using the word griot to call the African Canadian practitioners of the word, the editors of this volume tell us they believed that the Middle Passage did not destroy all the traditions of the captive Africans who were taken from their homelands, dragged across the Atlantic Ocean in the stinking bottom of slave ships, and made into slaves on New World plantations. It is this captivity of Africans and their dispersal throughout the world and the Americas that led to the formation of the African Diaspora that produced us-descendants of those who endured enslavement. Our ancestors lost much in captivity but not everything. In their heads they carried the words, songs, stories, poems, and their meaning. They remembered. And they passed on their remembrances to their children, and their children's children. And the traditions lived and flourished. And so the editors tell us that the griot tradition re-emerged on this side of the Atlantic, albeit in different shapes and forms.

Greater Toronto's modern day griots have taken on the roles of their ancestor-griots. They too are the keepers of law, tradition, and history. They too are the conscience of the community. They too use humour and morality to instruct, educate and entertain, even if they do it at a Kwanzaa inspired storytelling event, with a seven-piece reggae band, a hip-hop ensemble, or an intense pressure-cooking poetry slam!

There is more. This is the first time that an anthology focuses on black Toronto, and for good reasons. As black Torontonians we live the daily experience of police brutality, racial profiling, educational inequities, inadequate healthcare (including mental health) facilities, and other forms of discriminations. Marginalization is our daily fare. But we fight back. One of our main weapons is culture and art. We are empowered by the courage of General Tubman as she pushed through the undergrowth chanting down Babylon and singing liberation, by the warrior spirit of our Tutsi heritage, the dog-heartedness of the Yoruba captives who upon arrival to New World shores sharpened their machetes, and the fire-spitting tongues of the Mandingo *djelis* that accompanied Sundiata Keita in his battles to conquer evils on the plains of Kirini, Mali. Our Kirini is Toronto. Our conversations blaze fire under the heels of our oppressors and echo through our African Diaspora world from Toronto to Toledo, to Halifax and Havana, to Sénégal and Santo Domingo.

Hear these voices as they express our wanderings and wonderment as black subjects on a diasporic journey. See the poet leaping in the air at La Parole "as words pour from her mouth in flaming chants." Give ear to the cosmic chatter, Diasporic gossip, and revolutionary tales and dreams. Listen to these words as they utter in resonating dub.

It is with a generous heart that this anthology is offered. We say give thanks, give thanks to all the contributors, the editors, and all those who made it possible. And to the T-Dot, of course, for the inspiration.

Afua Cooper, the four-eyed griot
Toronto. Fall 2003.

What Makes Us Griots?

INTRODUCTION by STEVEN GREEN

"What makes you griots?"   A woman knowledgable about the tradition asked me as I hustled to promote the project, handing her a flyer with our information on it. The question is innocent enough, but is pregnant with a hidden antagonism. I know because I've asked myself the same question with that self-doubt and self destructiveness that plagues all people straddling cultural divides, in my case, the Canadian, Jamaican, and African conundrum. What gives you the right to be you? To walk, talk, think, wake up as you are? What gives you the right to exist? As with most simple questions that demand complex answers, it is a question I found myself asking over and over as the project unfolded. The question echoed in my mind because it is so central to the issues this anthology explores. In many ways, it is the perfect place to start this body of work. At its simplest, the question asks "what is a griot?" In what way do we — the artists in this book — represent that reality. At its most antagonistic, the question asks "what validates your claims to be part of the griot tradition?" "What gives you the right?"

Griots: Definitions and Inconsistencies
The first consideration when examining the question is the disparity of the term griot. In the African continent, the term griot is the subject of much debate. Origins of the word are unclear. Many Africans reject the term as they believe it is not a word belonging to any of the African languages. It is most widely believed to have French origins, but some believe it is Spanish or Portugese. Still other theorists claim the word did originate in Africa among the Mande, Wolof, or Fulbe ethnic groups. More than likely, due to the colonial imprint left on African soil, it is a combination of African words misinterpreted and mispronounced by the Europeans who encountered them. Since most historical documents available in Canada are of European origins, it is likely that what we call these artists is a misrepresentation of the true origin and terminology.

If people do not argree on the origins of the name, how can we agree on a standardized set of practices or define who or what a griot is? There are many names for the loosely related group of people we may generally refer to as bards or praise singers. Griot refers to artists, musicians, and singers who have the unique position in their community to inform, educate, and entertain.   Some of these praise singers are frowned upon and considered no better than professional beggars; something similar to what we might call buskers in Canada.   It would seem that griots have fallen out of favour; the practice performed by opportunists who sing praise for pay. Fela Kuti — the great Nigerian musician who created afrobeat music and is a revolutionary icon for blacks in Africa as well as in the Diaspora — was discouraged by his parents from becoming a professional musician for this very reason. In Niger in 1980,

Seyni Kountche, then president of Niger, suggested the term griot be changed to artist, musician, or singer, in an attempt by his government to clean up the profession. Opinions of griots change over time, as well as from region to region.

The Mande word for them is *djeli/djali,* the *Wolof guewel,* and the Fulbe *gawlo.* Each distinct region has a slightly different take on the profession than others. The tradition is most uniform in the western Mande region (northern Guinea and southwestern Mali). Go east or north, the practices and names change significantly. For example, the kora (the most complex and common instrument played by griots) is not played by the Senegalese griots. Parts of northern Africa, where they have artists who perform similar functions to griots are not actually referred to as such. So what makes African-Canadian artists griots, if people who share the same continent and are much more susceptible to cultural exchange, are not?

Geographic distance is one answer. Canada is far enough away that there is no conflict between our culture and say, one immediately adjacent. Use the United States as an example. There are many nations around the world who more wilingly embrace American influence than Canada. We are so close that we are in more danger of being swallowed up by American culture and values. However we can safely access cultural signposts that we believe are part of our African ancestry.

As people of the African Diaspora, we live in a cultural vacuum. Any cultural practices brought with us from the continent have either been erased or appropriated. The result is a loss of self and a constant yearning to reclaim our heritage. In the Diaspora, we search for corollaries and continuity that will tie us to such legacies. The movie *Roots* is a perfect example of this –the first place many of us heard of the term griot. *Roots* was an exploration of the author Alex Haley's personal history, told to him by a griot. It was the most popular television mini-series of all time. African Canadians crave connections with our ancestors and our history. The griot is a perfect vehicle to connect us.

Why? Inspite of the disparities surrounding names and popular opinion, the griot is the preserver and conduit of many imporant West African ideals. While there is no standardized set of practices for griots, many common functions performed by griots are represented in this book. They are considered historians and genealogists who recount their personal lineages and those of their leaders, maintaining the history of their communities. They function as advisors, a practice encompassing the much maligned praise singing. In its truest form, praise singing is meant to inspire the person or persons receiving praise to be at their best. The praise song may encourage governments to uphold promises to their people and keep warriors brave in battle when spirits are waning and begging for retreat. The tone of the praise singer seems to have taken a turn over the years. The late Fela Kuti was one of the most outspoken griots having used praise singing more critically than most. Kuti sang nationalist railings against Africa's corrupt colonial puppet governments (Nigeria's in particular)getting him arrested and beaten on several occassions. Decades later, the protest songs Kuti recorded in the 1970s are simply viewed as great music. However, we should not forget the true function of his powerful songs. Other outspoken griots include: Bob Marley and the Wailers in Jamaica, and writer-activists Wole Soyinka, Walter Rodney, and Assata Shakur who all suffered persecution for criticisms of their respective corrupt governments and societies.

The griot can occupy the mantle of teacher as well, giving instructions on better living. They also act as spokespeople, giving voice to members of their communities. The tools of empowerment are buried in traditional griot practices that griots in the African Diaspora willingly adopt. The table of contents separates the contributors' work into sub-groupings, showing how contemporary artists of the Diaspora perform such a traditional role.

So is this genetic? Beyond mimicking the continent and copying or claiming what we like from West African societies, as African descendents, there must be things that are simply in our bones. Call it instinct or natural law, there are some commonalities among African peoples that are hard to deny. You can almost look at it like a twin study. Two identical twins separated at birth move to opposite sides of the world and live completely different lives. Do they still walk alike? Sound alike? Do they still have similar mannerisms, personalities, and beliefs?

Not all the contributors to *T-Dot Griots* consider themselves to be griots, and others still had never heard the term before. We were pleased to learn that the griot manifests organically in Toronto without prior knowledge of the tradition. Quotations appear throughout explaining what the term means to the contributors. We encouraged them to answer as honestly as possible. We were not trying to win people over or force their words to support some thesis we concocted. Our interest lay in exposing authentic views about our lives in the African Diaspora. To some, the Diaspora may be a nebulous, unnecessary construction, and to others a very real, unifying element of black life. None of us is bound by any monolithic or singular ideal of what it is to be black, but there may be forces uniting African people on a spiritual level. Many submissions from artists who had never considered themselves to be griots, instinctually fit the template of the West African storyteller.

Straddling the Atlantic: The T-Dot Griot

Most of the artists in *T-Dot Griots* are first generation Canadians who, unlike many of their parents, did not choose to be here. Artists who are informed by the western world around them — speaking it's language and influenced by its principles — yet harking back in a spiritual, intuitive way to their ancestral African roots; a tapping in to the soul of blackness. As a launching point for this project we considered: what is that tapping in point for Toronto's young black artists? The artists represented in this book are not all aware of it, every one invokes the spirit of the griot. The unconscious, innate connection to the legacy is the most intriguing element of this project. The griot lives in our bones, and the griot is only one of many ancestors who inform our lives and our various Diasporic cultures. From Santeria to salsa to current slang, we are indebted to an ancestral spirit that acts upon us. As I read through the many submissions received from our contributors, I quickly saw how these artists fit into the griot tradition.

Griots have always existed outside of the caste system. The traditional griot occupies its own class. In many societies they do not marry non-griot members of society. When a griot dies, they are buried inside the trunks of trees, separate from members of the community. Over the years, the griot has gone from being a respected member of society's elite, to, in some cases, being considered "hired mouths" who sing the praises of important figures to gain favours, usually monetary. While the tradition retains much of its historical importance, the modern griot faces much ridicule from their contemporary societies. This scenario is eerily paralleled in Da Original One's "Can You Give Me a Dollar?", which expresses the trials and blues of being a storyteller and artist in Toronto. It also illustrates how many storytellers have accepted their fate as people on the fringe of traditional society, embracing the challenge to be revolutionary, uncompromising, and progressive in the interests of making their communities better. You'll witness this brave honesty in works like nah-ee-lah/naila belvett's "this is my rant" and Maki Motapanyane's "Had I Had Locks," which challenge the status quo of what a black woman is supposed to be with wonderfully liberating results. Sankofa Juba questions the political intelligence of war in "War.War.War.", and Yannick Marshall becomes the eyes, ears, and voice of Toronto's homeless in "We Slept in Chinatown." Our griots, however, are not partial to criticizing and tearing down – they also build up.

Griots use their songs to both inspire and motivate their subjects. They have long sung of the proud lineage of their people, keeping a mental record of important rulers and warriors and acting as historians for communities with little written history. The works of Kathleen James exemplify how modern griots meld the two worlds of written and oral history. Much of her work is informed by her academic studies, but is presented in an oral poetic form. Griots serve as a public conscience for their leaders, reminding them of the importance of staying noble and honest, even reserving the right to publicly criticize their leaders in the interests of the people. Such works as Al St. Louis' soaring "Heroes" and Christine Thompson's vivid "Trip to the Underground" are praise songs that inspire us today, by teaching about heroes of our not so distant past.

The griot is not limited to a static definition or a static group of people. Impressions of what a griot does for their society evolves with the society. Such shifting reality is the port of entry for the Canadian griot. Even though geographically removed from the continent, the spiritual connection continues. The credentials of a griot in traditional West African society were broadcast by the practitioner in a song recounting their lineage. Griots, just like many other trades, had their skills handed down from generation to generation by birthright. From this relationship, we can infer that many of us who came to the Americas, through the Middle Passage by way of West Africa, must share griot genetics.

The nature of the delivery itself is also a sign of our local storyteller's pedigree. The singing, theatrical nature of the griot translates into the dub poetry of naila/nah-ee-lah belvett, specifically her theatrical powerhouse *Stuck*; work that is beautiful on the page, but must be witnessed live for the full impact. Theatre has always represented a very important way to entertain and inform within African communities, and Jael Ealey's *My Upside Down Black Face* and Weyni Mengesha's *Lot.1975* tackle issues concerning our communities here in Canada.

In the area of criticism, there is a long history of "testifying" or "signifying" in North American griots. The artist as a mouthpiece of resistance with tongues as sharp as swords, is a cornerstone of our development. This is the act of addressing the wrongs or injustices within one's community and stating one's morality and opinion in a poem. This is often reinforced with wise principles learned from the community or the ancestors as exhibited in Nana Yeboaa's "The Calabash." Many artists speak out against the ills of Canadian society like Malik I.M. in "KKKanada" and Jane Musoke-Nteyafas' "She Wore." Others call humbly for healing like Kwame Stephens' "Prayer for the Black Child" and Dwayne Sewell's lamentation "A Still Small Voice in Gen-X."

Anthology (The Black Aesthetic Remix)

Through traditions such as call and response and signifying, artists are informed by the community around them. Engaged in an ongoing public dialogue with other artists. Hip-hop provides a strong example with KRS-One and MC Shan, Biggie and Tupac, Nas and Jay-Z. It was our goal to maintain that vibe and aesthetic with the anthology itself, not just the works within. We wanted the book to live, stepping out from the western academic form where most books thrive. *T-Dot Griots* is an appropriation and subversion of western academic devices.

We are improvisers, and spontaneous creators; off the cuff performers whose traditions are largely oral. However, it is necessary to permanently create a time capsule and a foundation that brings disparate artists together ina collaborative community. The works of Toronto's storytellers play together like a DJ set. The reader is a dancer hungry for the hits as well as the newest unheard gems, seamlessly mixed in a soul stirring journey with highs, lows, and surprising left turns. Expressive tales of Toronto are woven together allowing the artists within to speak to each other. Roots buried deep in African soil, T-dot's griots offer you an authentic view of life in Toronto from an African-Canadian perspective.

SHORT FICTION

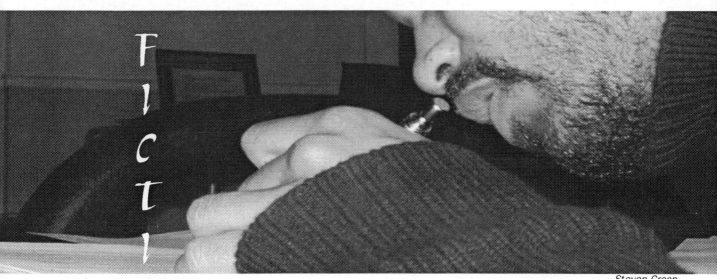

Steven Green

Introduction to Short Fiction

*B*edtime, quiet time or party time – the relaying of fictional stories in the African Diaspora is intrinsic to the culture. Fiction is a useful conduit of community values and ethics, often functioning as parables of wisdom. Aesop's fables and Anansi stories serve to pass knowledge from one generation to the next. Fiction can also serve to express one's place in society, culture, and community. 2002 Giller prize awardee, Austin Clarke encapsulates the mood of Caribbean immigrants as strangers in a strange land. His now classic "Toronto Trilogy" novels: *Meeting Point* (1967), *Storm of Fortune* (1971), and *The Bigger Light* (1975) make up a near archival memoir of Canada's first generation of immigrants from the West Indies.

The work of George Elliot Clarke, speaks to those black Canadians whose ancestry in Canada stretches back for generations. Born in Nova Scotia, his work is an insightful exploration of the history and traditions of Canada's oldest black communities. *Eyeing the North Star: Directions in African-Canadian Literature* (1997) – featuring many talented black short fiction writers from across Canada– greatly inspired *T-Dot Griots*.

Due to the importance of the written word in contemporary North America, what is written is often considered fact: It is critical that more black Canadian voices articulate their experiences in written fiction. Several artists are making their voices known; Makeda Silvera created Sister Vision Press, which began with the sole purpose of publishing the work of women of colour. Silvera is a powerful short story writer. Born in Jamaica, having spent the last 30 years in Canada, her work is an interesting melding of worlds. *Her Head a Village* is her most famous collection of short stories.

Using the veil of fiction, these artists are among the most prominent voices addressing issues affecting African-Canadian communities. Their wisdom is revered within their communities, and they are trusted to articulate some of the diverse needs and concerns of black Torontonians – spokespeople in the true griot fashion.

Plastique (Excerpt)

ZETTA ELLIOTT

"I thought you were staying longer this time." Rina opened the napkin on her lap and tore a slice of bread from the loaf in the basket. She spread a thick layer of butter to the very edges of the crust and then held the slice in her hand. Finding herself too nervous to eat, Rina set the bread down and looked out the plate glass window next to the table. "Yeah, well, I thought I'd be able to, but I can't." Meeting with Colin was a mistake. He was going to push her, she could tell. She took the bread up again.

"Can't or won't?" Rina bit into the tough bread and chewed slowly. Colin waited patiently for her to finish. "Can't or won't, Rina?"

"Look, Colin, I just changed my mind. It's still legal to do that in this country, isn't it?" Colin regarded her intensely for a moment.

"Sure."

Rina took another bite of bread. The butter felt thick and oily against the roof of her mouth. She hailed the waiter and asked for a glass of water. Her throat felt raw from the night before, strained from her efforts to talk over the music. Rina glanced up at Colin's hard, unyielding face. She had known him too well, too long. Marcia wouldn't push Rina if she sensed any real reserve. But Colin always lunged ahead, anxious to tear into her mind and uncover the truths he suspected were hidden inside. Completely open about his own life--his lovers, his politics, his likes and dislikes--Colin had little tolerance for the secrets of others. Even in high school, where their friendship began, he had picked at Rina. His tongue was like a delicately crafted hook: treacherously barbed, but gleaming and silver and nearly impossible to resist. Colin had learned early on that if he pushed Rina far enough, she would almost always bite.

"How was the club last night?"

Rina shrugged and avoided his eyes. "About what I expected."

Colin leaned forward, letting both his forearms rest on the table. "You're going to make this longer and more excruciating than it needs to be, Rina, if you answer my questions like that."

Indignation bolstered her failing nerves.

"Like what, Colin? We got in late last night, and I'm still a little tired, alright? I thought this was supposed to be a friendly lunch, not a damn inquisition." Rina felt Colin pull back.

"Well, maybe it'll help move things along if I tell you that Marcia called me this morning. And a couple of days ago, too. She's worried about you."

Rina rolled her eyes and tossed her crust onto the plate. "She's not worried about anything, and you know it. She's sick of me already--that's it, isn't it? I've pissed her off again and she wants you to take me off her hands. Well, I'll save both of you the trouble. I'm going back."

"When?"

"Today, if I can get a flight."

Colin sat back and tapped a staccato on the table with his perfectly manicured nails. "What makes you think she's mad?"

"Why else would she call you, Colin? If Marcia was really worried, she'd talk to me herself."

"And what if she tried but failed?"

Rina sighed and rubbed her eyes. Sometimes with Colin it was just best to give in. Give in early and let him have his way. He was right; it would be less painful this way. "Alright, Colin, I give up. What is it about me this time that's got Marcia all worked up?"

"She's your best friend, Rina. You could at least pretend that her feelings mean something to you."

Rina stared out the window and tried to look as though she hadn't been checked.

Colin studied her a moment longer and then began. "She's worried that you're having a hard time with things in the States. And she doesn't understand why you keep coming back–don't interrupt me." Colin's voice was low but firm. "Why you keep coming back when being here only seems to make you unhappy. Maybe you don't realize it, Rina, but you're not exactly a bundle of fun during your visits. You come back here looking all sad-eyed and lonely, and then you refuse to talk about what's really going on. I can't tell if you're upset by what you find here, or if you're just bringing something back from New York. But it isn't fair, Rina, not to the people who love you. Know what it seems like most of the time?" He waited for her to acknowledge him. Rina pulled her gaze back inside the restaurant and worked her face into an expression of curiosity.

"Most of the time it seems like you don't want to be here at all. It's like you've been drawn here against your will, summoned by some terrible authority that you despise and fear, but obey. People don't know how to act around you. They don't know whether you expect them to apologize for the way things are, for who they are. They try to ask you about your life down there, and you refuse to talk about it. Then you slam just about everything up here. The shopping, the nightlife, the men–everything south of the border is better somehow."

"I've never said anything was better, only different."

"Fine. Everything in your new world is different. But the effect is the same, Rina. You shut people out of your life. And for those of us who used to know you, that hurts." Colin stopped and forced Rina to look directly into his eyes. "She's hurt, Rina. That's why Marcia called me. Because she didn't know what else to do."

The waiter arrived and placed their steaming meals before them. Rina quickly picked up her fork and began to eat. The hot food burned the roof of her mouth but she continued to eat, determined to keep the space inside her and the space between them filled with something other than words. Colin watched her as his food cooled. When had things between them started to change? He'd been noticing it for a while now, since her last two visits at least. She's scared, he thought, terrified of some unnamable thing. Was it something foreign, or something familiar? By her downcast eyes and anxious mouth, Colin knew that right now Rina was also afraid of him. He had meant to bully her, force her to confront the situation between them. But this was something else, something more. He decided to take a gentler approach.

"What was the weather like when you left? Was it as cool as it is here? Lots of rain?" Colin kept his tone genuine but light. He looked at Rina for a moment and then started to eat.

Rina watched Colin furtively and tried to gauge his intent. Deciding it was safe to reply, she stopped wolfing down her lunch and toyed with her food instead, keeping her eyes on her plate.

"We haven't had that much rain; it's been kind of sunny, really." Rina glanced across the table. Colin seemed to be listening though occupied with his meal. She went on. "Spring comes a little sooner down there. It's funny, you know, they always talk about Canada like it's this vast, frozen territory. All snow and ice and igloos. And I keep telling them they're wrong, but it does feel colder here. And your leaves haven't started to bud. The forsythia are already out in New York. The cherry trees have all blossomed. The city looks beautiful in the spring..." Rina stopped, her voice close to a whisper. Had any of her words been audible? She looked up. Colin's mouth was full, but he nodded to show she still had his attention. Rina looked outside, cleared her throat and went on.

"It isn't that I don't expect there to be a difference between the two countries." She paused. "More than climate, I mean. More than the superficial things." Colin quietly asked the waiter for more water. Rina waited as her glass was refilled, then took a sip and went on. "That's one of the reasons I do come back. To see that difference. To remember. To be clear."

"Clear about what?"

"About my reasons for leaving. I guess sometimes I start thinking about my choices – when I'm down there, I mean. I get so comfortable sometimes, and then I start to forget. And so I come back here to remember." Rina smiled at her own strange language. "I'm not making much sense, am I?"

Colin grinned at the woman he was starting to recognize again. He tried not to rush her; he wanted her to open up at her own pace. "So coming back here confirms all the things you didn't like about Toronto."

"Ye-es, in a way, but–" Rina struggled to pull her feelings and ideas together. Where were the words she needed? "It helps me remember how I was living before, and it's just a lot of different things. I don't know if I'd say I get homesick, but there are things I miss about this place. Not necessarily good things, although there are those as well. It's just–" Rina faltered and searched for her meaning in the bland faces passing by. "It's like I need to come back here so I can keep going forward down there. Because sometimes it feels like I'm standing still. Can you understand that?"

Colin nodded but let her continue to find her words. "It's like I have to come back to make sure what I did was right. That troubles me more than anything else, really. To realize that my leaving didn't matter, didn't make a difference somehow. If I knew that my life down there was no different than the life I would've led up here... I don't know what I'd do, Colin. I have to know that what I did was right."

"Ok. I think I'm starting to understand."

"I wouldn't blame you if you didn't. Half the time I don't get it myself." They looked at one another and smiled.

"Is that really how you felt when you were here, Rina, like you were standing still? Your life always seemed full to me. You were constantly on the go."

The lunch crowd on the street outside thinned, and the restaurant began to empty. Rina searched the street in vain for a person like herself. "It wasn't so much about fullness – I mean, I was busy. I was working, I was doing things with my life. But–"

"But?"

"I just didn't seem to be getting anywhere. I couldn't see it, couldn't feel it. It didn't matter that I was here because I wasn't part of anything real. I've always wanted to belong to something, Colin. Something bigger than just a family or a group of friends, or a corporation, even. And I couldn't stand the smallness of this place. I couldn't stand the way that smallness pressed down on me sometimes. It was like I couldn't get up, couldn't expand, couldn't build anything great for myself. There was this ceiling and it weighed me down. Made me not even bother to try."

"The glass ceiling? You're talking about race." Colin was trying to stay with her, make her language more concrete.

"Yes, but it wasn't just a question of 'rising to the top.' It wasn't about my career. And this ceiling wasn't glass. It was this dull, heavy, cement-like thing. I could feel it hanging over me, even when I was lying in bed. It was like being trapped in an underground parking garage. Nothing but artificial light and endless circling, going from one level to the next without ever emerging into the world –the real world."

Rina looked out the window and wondered if she could offer a better explanation. Colin finished with his meal, and pushed his empty plate away. He seemed satisfied. Only a few tables around them still held diners. The wait staff had gathered at the bar to relax and await new patrons. Rina took a quick survey of everyone in the room. "Doesn't it ever bother you being the only black person in a room, Colin? Not seeing another black face on the street?"

He looked at her in surprise. "No, why should it? If I want to see black faces, I can go home and be with my family. It's not that big a deal."

"No, I guess not. Not for you, at least. But all of us don't have that option – of going home, I mean." Relieved to find her voice touched with envy and not malice, Colin prompted her to go on.

"Was that another reason? For your leaving, I mean. Toronto a little too snowy for you?" He smirked and expected Rina to smile as well. She surprised him again, however. Her face softened, lost some of its tension. When she spoke her eyes were remote, vaguely sad.

"I don't know why, Colin, but it matters to me. It really does."

The waiter interrupted their silence as he cleared the table and offered coffee or dessert. Colin looked at Rina. She shook her head and gazed out the window again, the growing distance between them widening her eyes. Uneasy, Colin searched for a way to bring her back.

"Have you seen your grandmother yet?"

Rina turned away from the empty, pristine street and nodded. "Marcia loaned me her car and I drove out there yesterday morning. She's fine. She asked about you."

"Is she still living on her own?"

As the restaurant door closed behind another pair of diners, Rina shivered, hugged herself, and rested her arms on the edge of the table. "Yep. Still fiercely independent. Wouldn't let me lift a finger while I was there. She sat me down on the couch, put an album in my lap, and we went through the entire family tree--again." Rina smiled and felt warmed by the recollection of her grandmother's pale, withered face. "After lunch she told me all about her latest crusade: the abolition of slavery in Africa."

Colin laughed and felt glad that their conversation had finally touched on a constant: Rina's grandmother never changed. She was forever taking up some cause, supporting her church's missions of mercy throughout the world.

"That's the Sudan, isn't it? I think I've heard about it on the news."

"Right. But like my grandmother says, charity starts at home. She was very concerned about the 'poor Negroes' living in poverty up in Harlem. No matter what I say, she just will not let go of that word. Drives me crazy. 'Dear, are there many Negroes living in your part of the city?' 'Yes, Grandma. There are lots of African Americans living in Brooklyn.' She just doesn't get it."

"Oh well, it could be worse. It's hard for them to give it up, I think, the older folks. It was such a step up at the time--what were they calling us before that? Cullud?"

Rina saw the word spelled out in her head, Canadian style: c-o-l-o-u-r-e-d. Mildly irritated, she shook her head and made the letters disappear. "And what do they call us now?"

Colin heard the edge in her voice. "Black, mostly. Although Afro-Canadian's starting to get a bit more play. Depends on the individual, I guess. A lot of people still identify with their place of origin." He paused and decided to pose a challenge of his own. "And what do you call yourself, Rina? Afro-American? Not Afro-Canadian, I bet. You were never especially patriotic."

Rina smiled wryly but said nothing. Emboldened by her silence, Colin went on. "I bet you're passing, aren't you?" He leaned back, pleased by his own ingenuity. "I bet you don't even tell people where you're from."

"Why should I?"

"Why should you, indeed. But I'm curious, Rina, doesn't your accent give you away? Or have you learned to adopt that charming American drawl?" Colin grinned spitefully and launched into a brief but loud impersonation. "How y'all feelin' today? Y'all want some mo' cornbread to go with that there fried chicken?"

Rina looked at him steadily. "No wonder they think Canadians are snobs."

"Oh, give me a break, Rina. Do they think you're a snob? Or have you managed to drop that, too?"

"Sure, Colin, whatever it takes. I also dyed my hair, changed my name, and tried to sell my Canadian passport."

"I imagine it wasn't worth much down there."

"On the contrary, it's worth quite a bit. People would give anything to live in a country with socialized medicine."

Colin leaned back in his seat and waited for the conversation to become serious again.

"Are you going to answer my question, Rina?"

"Which question was that, Colin? I thought we were trading national insults. What is it you want to know--what I call myself?" Rina shrugged, and kept her voice flat and indifferent. "Depends on the situation. Usually, if I'm asked directly, I'll say I'm Canadian. But people aren't always direct. Sometimes they ask, 'What are you?' And I generally lie. Not because I'm ashamed, but because the question itself is so absurd that it wouldn't mean anything to say, 'I'm Canadian.'"

"Why not? It's true."

"Of course, it's true, but the people who ask that question generally aren't looking for the truth. They're looking for confirmation. And that's what I try to give them. It wouldn't be an answer, really, to say I was Canadian. They'd only draw a blank-a big, white blank-and ask me something else in order to get around the lie. They'd say, 'Oh. But where are your people from?' And that's a more manageable question. I can have fun with that one."

"So where are your people from, Rina?"

"Same place as yours – the Caribbean." She paused, and let her lips curl in triumph and disdain. "And England, and Ireland, and America. Afro-America. You see, Colin, I don't have to pass for anything." Rina sat back and let her eyes slide from his face to the vacant world outside. "If you go back far enough, it's already there."

Neither bothered to break the silence that settled between them. The waiter approached their table and discreetly deposited the check, face down. "I've got it." Suddenly anxious to leave, Rina slid the white slip of paper toward her. She took out her most colorful American credit card and flashed it at the waiter who promptly returned.

Colin made a weak protest, then sat back, sullen, as Rina brought their encounter to a hasty and efficient close. "Guess I'll have to buy you lunch the next time you're in town." His gaze was heavy, designed, Rina thought, to weight her to the chair. "Any idea when that might be?"

The waiter returned. Rina signed the check and tucked her credit card back into her wallet. She pulled her scarf from her coat sleeve and wrapped it around her neck. "Some time this summer, probably." She held her coat, folded, on her lap. Colin still hadn't moved.

"Are you coming for Caribana?" His words were deliberate, slow.

Rina smiled but shook her head. "Not any more, I don't think. It's changed too much. I haven't had a good time at the parade since I was a child."

Colin looked at her, then out the window. "Everything changes, Rina." His eyes came back to rest on her face.

Rina wasn't looking for an apology and didn't appreciate being warned. "I know that Colin." She rose, slipped into her coat, and bent to kiss him on the cheek. Colin remained slouched in his seat; his eyes, heavy and black as magnets, were fixed intently on hers. Rina looked down at him with the calm assurance of impending liberty. She knew she could not be held.

"Aren't you going to say good-bye?"

Rina smiled faintly and brushed his hand with her chilled fingertips. "No need, I'll be back soon enough."

Colin dropped his eyes and looked out the window again. Rina followed his gaze.

"I guess there's no point saying anything if you don't really mean it. But I'm glad we had a chance to talk, Rina, you said some interesting things."

Colin stopped and gave her a chance to brace herself. Rina wished they could leave one another in peace, but knew the odds and their history were against her.

"Want to know what I think? Probably not, but I'm going to tell you just the same. After all, you can't always have your way. I think you should give all your fine words meaning and just stay down there, Rina. Open your eyes, choose a side, and just fall off the fence instead of riding the rail. Know what I mean?" He looked up at her with flat, unfeeling eyes. Rina felt the pull but wouldn't let herself give in. She wouldn't allow him to bait her this time. Rina pressed his hand, but like her fingers, her voice held no warmth.

"Good-bye, Colin."

Rina stood outside for a moment, unsure of her course. Behind her, the bells inside the restaurant door jangled, then became quiet. Rina buttoned her coat against the damp spring air and headed down the street, her pace fast and determined. Ignoring the pedestrian signals, she crossed the empty streets at will. Screw him, she thought. Screw Colin and everyone else who wanted to lock her in a box just to keep themselves safe. Rina ignored the flashing orange hand and stepped off the curb. She would not be held against her will. Nor would she permit anyone to check her anxious desire to roam. She would cross borders as heedlessly as she crossed these streets. She would always have the right of way.

Rina looked up and saw traffic clogging the intersection ahead. Yonge. She slowed her pace but reached the curb before the light had changed. Forced to wait, Rina glanced at the people around her but found no recognition in their eyes. In the dreary spring light all the faces looked ashen and dull. Occasionally a black face flashed in the street, but these too were wan and sapped of warmth.

Without furious motion to sustain it, Rina's anger began to recede. There was something in this city, in its clean, barren streets that calmed, tamed, numbed one's passions. What had she ever felt deeply here besides her anger and her fear? The light changed at last, and she moved with the crowd across the street. The swept pavement, hard beneath her heel, drew the last of Rina's fury from her body. She slowed and again considered where she was heading. Bay was next. Beyond that, she could not remember. The streets had never been truly familiar. Rina had always lived on the perimeter, the margins, at a distance from the city's softly beating heart.

The pulse had been weak by the time it reached the distant suburbs where she spent the first twenty years of her life. An agonizingly slow bus could take you to the eastern end of the metropolis; there, aside from the lake, the landscape changed completely, though the faces were mostly the same. It was a different world, really, a place apart with wide, quiet streets and broad stretches of lawn to separate the lovely people in their lovely two-storey, two-garage homes.

Even now, as a woman grown and in other ways so far removed from that scene, Rina couldn't help feeling that other world had not been real. And she knew that the city she named as her home, her place of origin, was not the same as the streets she wandered now. These streets she had only begun to know since her departure five years ago. She had to leave and come back -- it was the return that freed her, opened her eyes to small wonders and minor beauties she had never noticed before. The ugliness she had always seen, but that too could sprout anew.

Once she had returned for Christmas -- was it two years ago now, or three? Rina had been both startled and saddened by the scene that met her as she walked up Yonge Street. Missing the crispness of real winter air, she had decided to walk from the station instead of taking the subway to Marcia's. The length of one block told her she had made a mistake. The wind that night whipped through the corridor of glassy skyscrapers and bit cruelly at the skin on her face. Rina remembered jamming her hands in her pockets and clenching her gloved fists in an attempt to fight the piercing cold. She had tucked her head down and buried her face into her woolen scarf as best she could, but still the night wind sucked tears from her eyes, blurring the sharp white glare of holiday lights. Rina could remember how she had tried that night to count out the blocks as an icy trickle streamed down both of her cheeks, wetting her cold earlobes.

And it had been there, as constant as the wind, the chorus of voices struggling to rise above currents of frigid air to reach the ears of passersby. Like Rina, most people walked quickly, heads down, ears and mouths sealed by toques, earmuffs and scarves. But Rina couldn't help seeing the bare, outstretched hands reaching up to her from the pavement. They were there in every doorstep, on every corner, huddled in cheerless pools of light cast from the lamps above.

This was something new, a truth the city had never shown her before. Eyes made colorless and wet by the wintry air seemed to soften around the edges as the change fell from her hand. God bless you, miss. Were they Maritimers? No one in Toronto had ever spoken to her that way. God bless you, young lady. It was the first time Rina had ever heard those words. Over and over the blessings fell, but by the end of the second block her pockets were emptied. No more thick American quarters, no golden loonies, and she didn't really have bills to spare.

By the third block Rina surrendered and fled from the merciless weather into the warm, dark recesses of a cab. Fighting the wind for three city blocks had drained her, but so had the sprouting hands, reaching up at her from the cold cement sidewalk: open, hopeful, humble. Wrapping tight like a blush-white rosebud around a fat nickel, or Lincoln's coppery head. What's happening to this country? Rina had asked the question of herself and half-listened to the driver as he insisted that they were lucky because at least this year there wasn't much snow.

No, this was not fertile ground. Rina stopped and looked up at the blue street sign: University. Didn't that mean she was close to a park? She turned left and headed toward the leafless trees in the distance. Queen's Park. Rina smiled faintly as she remembered the words of an American friend. "Canada. You all have some pretty money. But why's that old lady's face still on every shiny penny?" Rina had found herself in the rather embarrassing position of being unable to explain the tie -- there was a logic somewhere, wasn't there? Something to do with the Commonwealth? Her friend was not convinced. "You all should take a vote, like those Aussies. Didn't they vote her out? 'Course you could have taken our side when you had the chance..."

And they laughed. "But then I wouldn't know all the words to 'God Save the Queen,'" Rina countered.

"True, and you wouldn't buy groceries at a store called Dominion with all that pretty play money of yours. Our greenbacks may not be much to look at, but they're strong. And I'll take strength over looks any day."

Rina could not remember if she had an answer to that, but suspected not. After all, what could she have said? She didn't miss the money, the crisp rose, blue, and lilac bills that bore the image of the fathers of confederation. Confederation...what was that date? 1867 came first to her mind, but Rina dismissed it as belonging to the Civil War. She had never been good with dates, but wished now that she had taken at least one Canadian history class in college. How could they let you graduate from university without knowing a thing about the country's roots?

Rina slowed and looked over her shoulder at the stony, closed-faced building across the street: the Royal Ontario Museum. Perhaps an ideal place to loiter, to spend the remains of an afternoon lingering amongst the ghosts and treasures from the nation's past. But it was Monday – would the museum be open? For her, probably not. Feeling cynical and petty, Rina pricked at her burgeoning idealism until it deflated and lay limp in her mind. What difference would it make, a collection of artifacts, or a list of dates? No difference at all, because the history was always the same: silent, vacant, corrupt. Rina continued heading south.

And she was mistaken, there had been a class – just one – at the beginning of her high school career. What had they taught her? Nothing of herself. Nothing of her people who came to this country long before confederation had passed. Nothing the isolation and cruelty that met the weary sojourners, of the coldness in a land and its people that pushed so many back to the country they had fled. Push-pull. That's what they had taught her. Push-pull. Two headings at the top of her page, and two lists of factors underneath. What pushes a person to leave her country, and what pulls her to another land? Push-pull made her think of her childhood: tug of war but the rope was a rag doll, and beneath was not mud but the ocean, shaded in blue like her teacher had told her. Red dotted lines where the borders should be.

What had they taught her? That Canada was a land of freedom? That Canada welcomed people from all over the world? Had they ever said a word about quotas? Had a teacher ever stood at the front of the classroom and admitted that slaves were beaten and sold on this side? The red dotted line stood for difference, isn't that what they had told her? The red dotted line kept us separate, contained all our goodness, repelled all the bad.

If ever she had believed this, Rina knew she believed it no more. Borders were purely symbolic, imaginary, hardly ever real. She thought of the scene in the club, of how American it had seemed: the music, the clothing, the dances, even the lewd gestures and thuggish posturing of the men. Rina had seen all of it before; it was foreign and yet all too familiar. It was there in her adoptive community, leering at her from stoops and street corners, oozing from the crowded clubs downtown. It was splayed across the pages of magazines, pounding from car stereos and portable radios. And each song conjured images from its accompanying video, a short film to document the fantasies of a few black men. The music, the lyrics, the images – all were on heavy rotation. No border could protect her from those. No border had ever really tried.

But was that really what she was seeking – sanctuary? Rina wasn't sure she believed in any destination where she would ever feel completely safe. By now the threat was global, and the threat had always been real. No, Rina didn't think she expected any country to make her personal security a national priority. She had grown accustomed to living with this jeopardy.

University split to encase the park. The scene was becoming more familiar. Hadn't they taken a trip once, as a class, to visit the seat of government? Rina thought she remembered endless, shallow steps and a foyer full of marble, but perhaps that had been the senior trip to Ottawa. Rina spotted some empty benches but followed her course around the park, her pace thoughtful and slow.

How many times had she been questioned, 'But what is it that you want?' Her answer had never been constant. Here, in this place, and at this particular moment, she would say she wanted to be cherished. Rina knew she would never be a national treasure, but what might it mean to be loved, truly wanted, not merely tolerated, pitied, or scorned?

She did and did not want to be petty. Rina knew she indulged herself too often, but these people had a way of provoking her, making her spiteful and ungenerous, unkind. Like the man with the baby carriage who had faltered at the elevator door. Rina's mind went back to that Christmas visit, that winter night when she fled the street and its pale, supplicating palms. She reached Marcia's building feeling grateful for the refuge, but also pensive and perturbed by the scene she left behind. When the elevator arrived, Rina leaned into a corner and stared absently at the buttons as she made her ascent. Almost immediately the elevator stopped, and the doors opened on the third floor to reveal a sandy-haired man standing behind a stroller. The first two wheels had already crossed the threshold when the man looked up and saw Rina in the corner. "Oh."

At first Rina was unsure of the sound – was it a sigh, a groan, a simple exclamation of surprise? A woman's voice called down the hallway

"Hold the elevator, dear."

Instinctively, Rina reached forward and pressed the button to hold open the doors. But by then the man had retreated, the carriage wheels were back on the hallway's plush carpet, and Rina realized at last that the "oh" was not language but punctuation, a period to end what he had begun.

Rina stood to her full height then, and stared in disbelief at her accuser. Just then a plump, red-cheeked woman joined him, and smiled warmly at Rina. "Thanks so much. Come on, honey, what are you waiting for?" Rina pulled back into her corner as the couple entered the elevator. The doors closed again and the young mother babbled cheerily at her baby. "Oh-" Rina had flashed her eyes at the woman. "Could you press 16 for us, please?" Rina had obliged, and used the moment to glance over at the man. His sandy head was bowed though he didn't seem to be watching the child, and his cheeks, like his wife's, were flushed.

The elevator reached the sixteenth floor and the couple got out, the husband more slowly than his wife. Before he pushed the last two wheels onto the carpet again, the woman turned back to Rina and wished her a happy holiday. Somehow, Rina had managed to smile before the doors slid back into place. She climbed the next eight flights alone, silently seething, daring the elevator doors to open and expose some unwitting victim to her rage.

But Rina had also been angry at herself. Why hadn't she recognized it? His look of blank refusal, the backward motion of his body as it instantly withdrew from her unspoken threat. And that sound, surely she had heard it before. Oh meant 'no, I cannot share this space with you; I've got to protect my child/my wallet/my virtue' – which contagion had he feared? No longer chilled by the wintry weather, Rina felt her palms moisten as fury boiled the blood beneath her skin. And only his wife had shamed him. Rina thought of the Americans she met who were so delighted when they learned where she was from. "Canadians are always so friendly, so polite." But those were foreigners, and they were white; there was no way for them to know the truth.

Rina continued heading south, leaving the park behind. This part of the avenue she remembered. When she was a child, the floats from the Caribana parade had wound this way. In those days the celebration had been real; no police barricades prevented revelers from flowing into the street and dancing alongside or on top of the flatbed trucks that carried the enormous, pulsing black speakers and the glimmering steel drums. Rina remembered the joyous motion, the swirl of sequins and bright colored feathers; the glitter that looked as though it had been sprayed onto the dancers' luscious brown skin. She still held a memory of being lifted onto one of the trucks by her father, of watching him emerge and disappear into the crowd as the vehicle surged and stopped, then moved ahead again. It was, perhaps, her best memory of the city. One day in a year when the streets were filled with black people, when the bleak grey concrete was obscured, enlivened by the magic, the life, the wonder of them all.

Rina stopped at a light and looked at the landscape ahead. A wall of skyscrapers blocked her view of the lake. It didn't matter. She couldn't walk there today, not if she was planning to catch an early flight. Rina crossed University instead. Alone on the concrete island, she sat down on a bench and wrapped her arms across her chest. The question resurfaced in her mind: what is it exactly that you want? She wanted another way of being. She wanted a life somewhere in this world where she wasn't already cast into a mold, cast for a role someone else had scripted.

This country was like a lover, and Rina, a woman scorned. The idea was absurd, but the feelings were almost the same. Rina hugged herself and traced parallels between the other relationships in her life that had similarly failed. The script was the same, but this one Rina had penned herself. I left you because you made me feel loveless, because you never looked at me with pure longing, only with revulsion or lust or not at all.

I left you because I hated the woman I became in your presence, the woman you expected me to be...

Rina looked up at the nearby statue, a monument to a war hero she neither knew nor admired. She addressed the rest of her speech to his deaf stone ears.

"I left because you were impassive, unresponsive, even sadistic and brutal at times. Because you held your arms open with promise, but never embraced me as your own. As my own. I was never your equal, or your darling. I was your debtor-imprisoned. You kept me apart from my people; you said if I loved you, I didn't need them.

"You cut me off from my stories, said they weren't authentic or as real as your own. You made me feel as though my very being were a present, a charitable donation you had deigned to bestow. But I don't need your magnanimity. I no longer need to search your eyes to find my true worth. Because you never really knew."

Rina looked down to the end of the street, to the place where the lake should have been.

"And now I've found another and perhaps he's no better than you. But he's the lover of my choosing and I love him precisely because of that choice. Though you have hurt me, I will always be tied to you. But I'm able to say by my leaving that I will never again feel bound."

Rina squinted slightly as the weak spring sun lit the grey-white sky. The problem was, she had found no one here nor there to whom she could say these things. Rina looked at her watch and sighed. It was time. She pulled herself up from the bench and continued heading south.

Shelley Winters

STEVEN GREEN

Winter whispers on white wings back to my youth. We standing knee-deep in white powder thick enough to make most major league cartels proud. We shiver like brand new babies delivered to this life cause hell yeah we were new. New to this game of Mom and Pop car jacking, as in, from your own Mom and Pop. Kirk put us on to Mark Murphy, who put us on to wild ways that never registered before in the backs of blank minds that read like empty billboards. Ryan, Bobby, Richard, Kirk, Cleveland and me stand with our bones vibrating some restless song. Like vibrating lips against a whistle. Think Bobby might actually have been whistling "Going Back to Cali" to keep himself warm. Our skins all goosed, while Mark tries to turn the engine over.

Cleveland pulls the garage door down locking the rest of us out. Straight nervous. Quick to hide our grand theft auto from prying eyes and Ryan's voice bumping his head back with:

"Your mom might be from Barbados but she's got one crusty Grenada here boy."

"Shut up. It's called a GRE-NAH-DUH dumb ass."

"Whatever."

By the time, it seems, Mark gets the engine on its side and back over, we're down the street. Too nervous to holla at young dimes that made a dolla cause Cleveland didn't wanna get caught. Fair enough. They were his keys and our dreams, sponsored by Mark Murphy's derelict mother who facilitated the brother's lack of conscience and overflow of confidence. Cleveland made us all promise to be confidants and not tell the tale we would all know so well; not knowing just how easy that would become.

The burbs burst by us like we were the ones standing still. Set the car in the parking lot in back of Mac's Milk. Old man Donato hooks us up like we'd won da Lotto, like late night Channel 47 Cable 4. In other words, we leave the store with dirty magazines and sticks on fire in our faces. Flicking off the flakes of our tender youth with each tap of ash that hits the snow. Huddle up around Mark Murphy for the next play on life. Behind Alton Towers cursing like we know what "Bumbaclot" means. I'd heard my uncle say it at a Thanksgiving dinner party the month before. Bobby bends over laughing off the giddy nerves flying up in us from being rebellious. Up on the tenth floor, the apartment thick with the smell of ripe banana and oxtail. But we're being pimped by the Big Mac and don't find that food appealing; except Mark Murphy who snatches a piece of breadfruit from up under some tin foil.

"Those are for my sister to take to work."

"She isn't going to miss one, guy."

"Got any peach schnapps?"

Flipping "Thriller" on 45 and dipping back into tracks beyond their sell by date in relation to our cool. While other brothers were getting cold. Down right cold as souls on ice and discovering other .45s that left less innocent crimes than those we committed on PA days that never went public. Making deposits on snow banks behind the building,

"Snowball battle royale!"

Every crevice between layers in our barriers caked with wet snow, melting from our sweat, panting hot steamy breath into the air. Pile drivers performed without license, invitation, or provocation. Mark and Ryan roll down hill. We all join the pile up. Our voices splatter up against that hollow sky you get at dusk in mid-winter. Deep enough to keep a thousand secrets.

Our avalanche uncovers a dead body fossilized to the hillside. Twisted like a weathervane, a bullet removed the left side of his brain. His eyes wide open, staring at us from a place somewhere in our futures. His mouth is open and his words are snatched away. Time stands still as all we can feel is the chattering whisper of naked branches in the wind.

The seasons turn over like that dusty old car engine. We'd been caught. Ryan wouldn't shut his damn mouth. Cleveland never got his driver's license until he moved out. Mom had me on whistleblower, ratting out the block and the nearest smokes providers to the kids under the age of 18. Mark Murphy's cool dissipated with the coming heat of spring. Moved out to the States to live with his dad who'd made his mom the derelict she had become. Truth came out years later how Ryan's mother found out about our snow day route, when Ryan stopped eating and started sleeping in her bed at night.

To this day bredren, that's the only dead body I've seen. Funny enough he never turned up in papers. Now the death toll of young black men in our community has skyrocketed to over 100 in the last five years and every other day I see a new face in the *Toronto Sun*. Staring back at me in place of that nameless face buried in a brutal winter funeral on the hills we took for granted as safe. I see that face and wonder what words had been stolen from his open mouth, whenever winter whispers on white wings back to my youth.

Deportee

WENDY VINCENT

I'm on my way to Jamaica, October 2002.   My favourite and sole surviving uncle on my father's side of the family passed away after succumbing to illness from days of flu like symptoms.   I miss Yard badly and this is a bittersweet sojourn for me.   At the airport I am struck by my feelings of loathing, pity and pride as I sit in Terminal One's departure lounge with a shipment of farm labourers, returning to Jamdown after a spell of work somewhere up north. I hate that there are no jobs in Jamaica for these men to be employed.   I can only imagine their families bursting with anticipation to see them back home and the support they so desparately need from their poorly paid work, cultivating apples on some Niagara region based backra's farm.   Doing work that none of the locals deem worthy of their effort. I hate that somehow a trade agreement was drafted to make these men 'fair trade'.   It is 2002 and there is no overseer at the helm of my airplane, but as I watch these young men — roughly the same age, skin tone, and even size — I swear I can smell the stench of post colonial, millenial, northern North American slavery wafting from them.

Upon arrival in Jamaica, threats of tropical storms "Lily" and "Isidore" and other sisters of Mother Nature just behind, were giving locals the chills and bad Hurricane Gilbert flashbacks.   I had truly come home in the midst of hurricane season and election time.   One of my first stops on a quick round-a-bout of new Kingston was a new attraction known as Emancipation Park. I honestly don't recall what the land was used for previously and I looked forward to seeing the dedication to the 40th anniversary of Jamaican Independence in all its splendour.

While my aunt navigated her vehicle in the parking lot, a young homeless man rushed up in the rearview mirror.   He waved wild signals to my aunt so she could properly slip into the sole space available in the lot.   I recall that while this brother was conspicuously homeless, he was not particularly destitute looking.   I'd already seen a few downtrodden brothers in the day that I had been around.   The moment my aunt clinched the spot and the successful taxiing was complete, the young man offered his hands in the gesture of a beggar and asked us for money.   My aunt rolled down her car window with the passenger side to the curb.   My senses were immediately paralyzed by a familiar sounding voice speaking words so terribly unfamiliar.   This beggar was no Yardie.   He was Canadian. Like an invisible hand pinning me to my seat, I was riveted as he told his story of life as a deportee, and how he became a beggar in Jamaica.

As we emerged from the car, I was struck by the destitution of Jamaican beggars.   My mind was still downloading the barefoot, raggedy pants, matted haired and glazed eyed sufferer I had seen earlier in the day.   T'ings are well rough in yard, but as I recalled stepping on sleeping bags and food remnants of folks who sleep outside of St. Andrew subway station in downtown Toronto, I couldn't help but think of the cruel universe of homeless life.   The young man who stood in front of me now proved to be a very different species among Jamaica's homeless population.   When he opened his mouth to thank my aunt for the money she had put in his extended hand, I was immediately struck down by his words.   The strongest Canadian accent came out of his mouth.   The strongest Canadian accent I'd heard since listening to my own voice against all the Jamaican tongues.

He told us his name was Chris and thanked us for our offering.   My aunt asked how he came to be a homeless beggar in the streets of Kingston, Jamaica.

I DID SOMETHING I AM NOT PROUD OF…
NIGHT CLUB…CANADA
GUN… SHOOTING…
DEPORTED…
CAN'T ASSIMILATE INTO JAMAICAN LIFE…
NO RELATIVES…
INTERVIEWED ON RADIO JAMAICA…
SLEPT AT THE AIRPORT FOR DAYS AFTER I ARRIVED…

"Jesus."   Eventually I spoke, though I was hesitant at first.   When I did, Chris immediately stood rigid with recognition.

"Where are you from?" he asked.

"Canada."

"Where in Canada?" his questions turned to rapid fire. He locked eyes with me as though he'd been reunited with a long lost relative, unfound since he was first shipped off to Jamaica.   He started randomly roll calling street names "Oakwood! Vaughn! Midland! Sheppard!", and neighbourhoods "Regent Park! Brampton! Scarborough! Jungle! 'Ssauga!,"   like they were the names of his children.

It's a blur five months later, but he lowered his voice and whispered the details of the event. The night he shamefully walked into California Dreams on Peter Street with a gun in his coat pocket and how he went from driving through the streets of Toronto to begging for money in Kingston's.

Though Chris's story differs from the gang affiliated gun men being flown back to Yard on a regular basis, it is not unique.   In addition, his squatter's residence — an abandoned bus in Emancipation Park — is uptown real estate relative to the other spots throughout Kingston.

Chris has been gone from Jamaica for so long that there is no trace of the world famous Jamaican accent.   More over, there was no one in Jamaica for Chris to reconnect with once he returned to the island.   He left for Canada at a very young age and there was no reunion or address in Jamaica awaiting his arrival.   As a consequence, his first nights of sleep before ending up on the streets were on the actual Norman Manley airport compound.

Chris went on to explain that in addition to not having any relatives to speak of, he could not blend into Jamaican culture.   Truly a stranger in a strange land.   Flashback to the farm workers with whom I flew to Jamaica that very afternoon.   Black Jamaican men who's solution to the job shortage was to loan themselves to Ontario's agricultural industry.   There was no work for Chris.   He talked of the problems locals had in understanding the way he spoke and how people were constantly asking him if he was Haitian or African; ethnicities on the low end of Jamaica's social totem pole.

      Fast forward to February 2003.   I wonder if Toronto Police Chief Fantino had an opportunity to visit Emancipation Park and if he and Chris or any other deportees crossed paths.   Stories of gunmen who melt back into the fabric of Kingston gangs and Jamaica's crime population are easily found, for they are full of sex appeal.   But between the hardship of Chris' situation and the rent-a-slave farm workers, Fantino could not have seen the Jamaica I see during his trip.   Especially if he refuses to acknowledge the racial profiling and continues to scuttle the debate on police conduct towards the black community.

Unnatural Instinct

Karen Richardson

    Blake looked up in disbelief from seventeen floors below. There she was standing on the ledge for the third time in as many months.

    "It hasn't rained in two weeks. That's gotta mean something." Astra shouted at the top of her lungs. "It's not worth it, Blake. It's not even worth it."

    Blake shaded his eyes with his right hand to avert the mid-July sun. Squinting, he gasped as Astra barely concentrated on her footing, while scaling the aluminum siding like a backward Spiderman.

    "Astra honey, why do you have to do this?"

    A small crowd of passersby began to assemble.

    "This life is unnatural Blake. I just want to get back to nature...to return to the mother of us all." Both frightened and embarrassed, Blake clenched his banana box of discount groceries and headed into the elevator. 'Good Gracious. Why does she insist on putting me through this? I told her we could start making some changes in the fall. I told her to be patient' he thought.

    The elevator seemed to stop at every floor. Seven. Eight. Nine. The door opened revealing a heavy-set European woman and her pre-teen son.

    "I'm going up!" barked Blake.

    "Rosario, why you push all da button for?" The woman scolded the boy, slapping his hand. "You bother the nice man."

    Blake stood stiff as a rootsman at a rave, staring at the numbers as they lit up. Ten. Eleven. 'I wonder if she's still out there?' Twelve. Thirteen. 'Is this milk leaking?' Fourteen. 'What if she...?' Fifteen. Sixteen. 'Please God, let her be inside.' Seventeen. He darted down the hall to the right, his forehead dripping beads of sweat and pushed through the unlocked door to 1708.

    "Astra! Would you get in here please?"

    "One sec. I just have to water the Alfalfa."

One soiled sock appeared in the window sill. In comes Astra in a beaded paisley wrap and a Che Guevara T-shirt, hair tied back with a bandana.

"Punishment, I say. The earth is being chastened for these unnatural ways. Not a drop of rain so far this month. Can't even trust the Almanac this year." Astra swooped in to give Blake a kiss and remove his tie.

"What, is that milk on the floor?" Astra leaves the empty juice jug in the sink before reaching for the mop.

"For goodness sake! It was leaking!"

"Oh Blake, milk comes from cows, not four litre bags. Just another sign its time we leave this place. The city is no place for people to live, you know."

"Yeah, I know."

Astra could never thank her Yogi enough for that revelation. Since her final class last March she had developed a passion for subsistence farming; growing a variety of Asian vegetables and fad cooking herbs in terra cotta pots outside the bedroom window.

"The Universe wants us out in the country Blake. We're not city people."

Blake rolled his deep brown eyes before bursting open a bag of chips and turning on the tube. He'd channel his chi right through Yogi Sharma's jaw if he was a fighting man. After all, he and Astra were from the city, born and raised. Regent Park to be exact. Best friends since the fourth grade, then high school sweethearts, college kindreds and now estranged husband and wife. The city had been just fine for them until Yoga season started. Blake and Astra weren't your average residents of Canada's oldest housing project, so they were pretty ecstatic about landing a lake-view apartment in the Cityscape Co-op.

"Chips are unnatural too, babe." Astra grabbed the half-empty bag of dill pickle and tossed it out the window.

"Pickles are preserved cucumbers, a dwarfed variety actually."

"Good grief Astra, why'd you do that? You can eat your wheat gluten and I'll eat my chips, thank you." Says Blake after sucking his teeth in disgust.

"Oh no-no- no you won't. You can't kiss me with greasy lips. Differently, I'll leave you. You wouldn't risk that, would you? All those fat substitutes cause anal leakage. Maybe you should do an herbal cleanse. Rid your system of all that fatty Caribbean food you eat."

She seems happy these days. Astra normally appears so uncomfortable in her own skin. So, despite the ongoing battle, Blake is pleased that she's finally got something to be excited about. He fears, however, Astra may be losing herself in the process.

"And the TV. Pure fantasy. I'm gonna donate it to the woman's shelter once I disconnect the cable. Try reciting mantras, babe. It'll help you relax."

Blake got up annoyed and walked to the bedroom. He dove butt first into the opium bed where he had a great view of a struggling pot of sage.

Astra's never been this at ease before, though she always seems dissatisfied with anything resembling her former self. As teens, the pair was labeled 'whitewashed' since Blake always had his nose in a math book and Astra was too posh to admit she lived in The Park. Her caucasian friends from the School of the Arts never got to meet any of her neighbours. She made sure of it, jumping on the subway after class for one stop while the rest of the Regent Park youth would walk the eight blocks home. The neighbourhood kids had her mistaken though. Astra never wanted to be white. She just didn't want to be 'ghetto'. In fact, being African was something she used to celebrate in her paintings. 'I can't believe this. My girl thinks she's Old McDonald on Queens Quay.' Blake got up to move the plant out of his line of vision. 'She must be losing her mind'.

"Shanti Ommmmmm…come and join me Blakie, you'll like it." Astra called from the living room; sitting cross-legged on the neutral rattan rug, hands resting at her knees index to thumb. Astra wants to move out to the country now. Caledon or Peterborough, maybe. Somewhere she can do cartwheels and see the stars at night. Somewhere she doesn't have to grow organic veggies on the ledge.

"Sorry Astra, last time I repeated those words I was jumping up to some Lord Shorty tune at Caribana."

Blake lay on his back thinking.

'We're not in the ghetto anymore, not even on social assistance.'

Astra leads watercolour classes at the centre for battered women. Blake has a good accounting job. Just one more exam to complete his CA. The only reason they managed to land a suite in the co-op is because their names had been on file with Toronto Public Housing since birth.

Blake hardly believes moving to the sticks will satisfy Astra for any length of time. How would she get around on her bike out there? The local folk probably don't even have an authentic Hindu yoga instructor. What's worse, their neighbours might not like the scent of dhoop sticks. Astra's fickle. Even New Age Black Barbie will eventually go out of style. Blake focused hard on that revelation. He prayed silently as Astra meditated in the next room. Perhaps she would truly find clarity this time.

Blake wasn't so sure how to relate to his wife these days. She seemed so content in her world of culturally appropriated values and practices. Therein her nappy tresses could flow, wild and free.

"Blake," laughed Astra, now standing by the bedroom door "that's not how you do it. You should be sitting with your back straight. You ought to give Yogi Sharma a try."

Blake shook his head, hoping Astra would just leave him be.

"See Blake, we really do need to get away. Look how unhappy you are. This life we've got here, it's just not natural."

Blake let out a sigh as Astra placed the potted sage plant back out the window.

"No it's not, baby. None of this is."

V
I
S
U
A
L

A
R
T
S

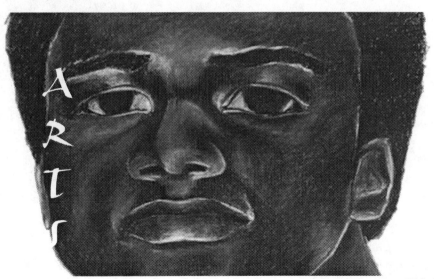

"Cool Pose 8.b", Charcoal on Canvas, Sandra Brewster

Expression In Images

JACQUELINE COHEN

Images often express what words do not.   Look around. There are endless stories in the visual forms we see that are taken for granted — images that define a culture and a people.   The Egyptians are noted for their pyramid structures and hieroglyphics.   Just as one look at a jade sculpture or rice paper drawings automatically takes one's mind to Asia, we obtain an instant understanding of an entire culture or moment in time with a single glance.

"Serenity" by Tricia Douglas

We may not be fully aware of the symbolism behind the images we see, however we can in many cases identify where they come from and have an experience with them without the use of words.   In North American society, images are commonly used to sell products, ideals, and dreams.   In our free market society, this example emphasizes the importance of images and their power.

From the first primitive images found in caves to the present day billboards and galleries, images have played a valuable role in documenting current events and cultural ideals.   Artists are entrusted with the significant responsibility to creatively document and interpret from their perspective their surroundings and the existing cultural landscape of their time.   It is especially critical that artists of African descent adhere to this mandate. If we chose to allow others to depict us, we may only be left with brutal images such as the beating of Rodney King* and the disempowering images of Dwain Alexander Lawes.**

As founder of the Power of Expression Art Auction™, I made a commitment to promote artists' work, to the best of my abilities, through the use of greeting cards.   Realizing that not all art work is suitable for greeting cards, I came up with a plan to share the art and artists with the public.   My secondary goal was to heighten the profiles of my artists and my company. That plan became the Power of Expression Art Auction. In my years in the business of art, I have come to learn that collectors will invest in what they enjoy and believe in. They are making an investment in our community, our identity, and our culture.

As black Canadians, we are obligated to write our history from the perspective of our experiences. Toronto's own black visual artists have begun to write the cultural history of who we are and what we believe in. Together, they are working towards increasing our sense of identity and spreading the beauty of our culture to other Canadians and to the world.

"Gathering" by Tricia Douglas

Photo journalist, Tricia Douglas is capturing our image in daily life. Artist Robert Small, very much a storyteller with his own charcoal renderings, documents history in the making and history already made. From its inception in 1993, the Official Black History Month Poster is produced annually. Stephen Taylor replicates the historical photographic images of our ancestors. These artists together with several others are making history, documenting our past and securing our future.

African-Canadian art makers generally acknowledge that something wonderful is happening here in Toronto. People from all around the city are coming together to celebrate African-Canadian culture created by black artists. Events such as the Power of Expression Art Auction celebrates visual art, as well as creating a marketplace where it can be purchased. Every year for the past five, people have attended the auction with the intention of viewing and buying art.

The auction grows each year. The attendance has risen significantly since it began in 1997, with sales quadrupling. To date, approximately $80,000 in art has been sold through this forum. In 2001, the Our Image Visual Arts Awards were introduced. The awards were designed to publicly recognize the accomplishments of professional artists and their work. To be able to add the awards to the auction after only 3 years, speaks not only to the development of this event, but also to the interests of individuals in the city of Toronto.

Several other art events are regularly hosted with the same goal in mind; to increase awareness of the importance of visual art created by the African Canadian community. The Human Rights Commission hosts an annual Black History Month Art presentation. For the entire month of February each year, Human Rights Through Art displays the work of local artists. Wedge Gallery hosts an annual photography show with the works of local and international artists. Several of the local artists actively show their work in independent and group shows throughout the year. When the next generation looks at their surroundings, they will see images that celebrate who they are thanks to the contributions of Toronto's black artists.

---

*Victim of police brutality on March 5th, 1991. Four LAPD officers stopped King who had been, by their accounts, driving recklessly and resisting arrest. They delivered 56 baton blows and 6 kicks, which resulted in 11 skull fractures and kidney damage. The acquittal of all four officers in the April 1992 trial sparked the South Central riots that followed the verdict. Two of the four officers were eventually convicted.

**Robbed a Brampton Toronto Dominion bank with four accomplices, January 11th, 1992. Nancy Kidd, an employee at the bank, was shot and killed by one of Lawes' accomplices, his cousin Marlon Rowe. Lawes claims to have been under the influence of a voodoo priest, Rhyll Carty, who he asked for protection from the police.

THEATRE

"I write so that these words/thoughts won't own me anymore"
– nah-ee-lah/naila belvett, poet, playwright

Scene from 'da kink In my hair' l to r: Quancetia Hamilton, Miranda Edwards, Ngozi Paul, Raven Dauda, d'bi.young, Ordena Stephens

Introduction to Theatre

*I*f all the world's a stage, Toronto is no exception. Theatrical performance is integral to griot artistry because it encompasses all other forms of black storytelling: music, acting, story, poetry, etc. Many artists in Toronto either draw from or actively participate in theatre. Much of Toronto's black population has roots in the West Indies, where there is a great theatrical history in pantomime and other stories for the stage. These influences contribute to Toronto's on-going relationship with theatre.

In Canada, black theatre has gone through periods of growth and recession. The longest running company in the country is Montreal's Black Theatre Workshop. Formed out of the Trinidad and Tobago Drama Committee in 1972, Black Theatre Workshop has been a cornerstone in presenting Canada's most prominent black theatre artists. They have produced important Canadian works including Djanet Sears' *Afrika Solo*. Along with Toronto's own Black Theatre Canada which closed its doors in 1988, Black Theatre Workshop has proven something of a breeding ground for Toronto's theatre scene.

Djanet Sears has gone on to critical success with Obsidian Theatre Company and their co-production with Nightwood Theatre of Sears' *Adventures of a Black Girl in Search of God* (Harbour Front Centre 2002). Headed up by Allison Sealy-Smith, Phillip Akin, Djanet Sears and a host of Toronto's most talented actors and directors of the Diaspora, Obsidian has their sights set on using their extensive knowledge of theatre to introduce a mainstream audience to the canon of the black arts community. This commitment afforded Obsidian the honour of being the first ever Canadian company to produce Pulitzer Prize winning African-American playwright August Wilson's *The Piano Lesson*. As well as bringing internationally celebrated work to black Canadian audiences, Obisidian is committed to developing new works by Sears, Cheryl Bogle, Joseph Pierre, and other contemporary playwrights. Sears' own anthology *Testifyin'*, now in its second volume, is an excellent source for more in-depth information –as well as excerpts from– Canada's talented black playwrights.

ahdri zhina mandiela's b current brings a vibrant dub poetic style with an emphasis on developing young voices. mandiela's company remains connected to her Jamaican roots and her background as one of Toronto's premier dub poets, all the while illuminating the complex Diasporic experiences of black Canadians. d'bi.young and nah-ee-lah/naila belvett's *Yagayah*, as well as belvett's *stuck* (an excerpt of which is included in this anthology), are two excellent dialogues on being black in Canada. Many of Toronto's new crop of talented theatre artists have done work with b current, including actor/writer ngozi paul, director Weyni Mengesha, and musician True Daley.

While all of these companies employ elements of traditional African storytelling, the AfriCan Theatre Ensemble's mandate is to bring African stories to Canadian audiences. Established in 1998, Artistic Director Modupe Olaogun has produced African themed shows from Ola Rotimi's *Our Husband Has Gone Mad Again,* to Ama Ata Aidoo's *Anowa*, a play about a woman turning her back on the traditions of her Ghanaian community and seeking her independence.

Nia

(Excerpt from *da kink in my hair*)

TREY ANTHONY

NIA: Sandy held her breath, when you pulled back the blanket. Pity she didn't pass out, while you were looking it all over. I'll always remember how you smiled when you looked at his ears, then laughed out loud when you saw his pale fingers. Sandy knew it was good, and she had passed again. (*beat*) I couldn't believe it. Couldn't believe she was back on her pedestal. (*Laughs bitterly to herself*) Yeah you knew she had skipped more classes than she had ever gone to, hung out with the wrong crowd. Dropped out of high school because she was pregnant. But you conveniently forgot all of this because she had given birth to a bundle of brown joy. (*2 beats*) Her kid's hair was so wavy; I thought you would jump right in for a swim. You were such a proud grandmother. Quickly calling all the family and telling them how the baby could easily pass for white. (*Shakes her head in disbelief*) And I just wanted to go over there and smack you in your damn black ugly face, and ask you, what about me?!

What about Tasha? Did you know that her kindergarten teacher said she's reading at a grade two level, and today she tied her shoelaces all by herself? But you wouldn't give a damn, would you? Because you can't find a wave in Tasha's hair. No good hair, no mistaking my baby for white. Her skin is black coffee, black coffee without milk. And I know it's all my fault 'cause I chose to lay down with a man that if he closed his eyes and didn't smile you would have thought he left the room. (*beat*)

Midnight you called him, but personally I think he looks more like quarter past. When Tasha was born you marched over to the hospital, hoping for the best but expecting the worst. And you got that didn't you? You didn't laugh when you looked at Tasha's dark fingers and even darker ears. Your face said it all. No need to speak mom, because I had heard it all before. (*Imitating her mother*) "How many times do I have to tell you girls pick the men you lie with, anything too black is never good." (*Pause*) Anything too black is never good? I should have known that because I was never good enough for you was I?

You hated my blackness. Ranted and raved every Sunday afternoon as you heated up the pressing comb to press my bad hair while Sandy ran outside, the good hair one. We stayed in the hot kitchen and I pinned my ears back holding my breath, not daring to move because I didn't want to get burned again. And as you fried and cooked my bad hair, you cursed my blackness. You cursed my father, hating to see him in me. (*2 beats*)

You know, I'm 32 years old and I still cry when I see little black girls in red ribbons. You wouldn't buy me them. You said I was too black to wear red. No little red dresses or red socks. 'Cause I was too black for red (*Getting emotional*). Too black to wear red? And you know last week I bought Tasha 14 red ribbons and put all of them in her hair, yep, all 14 of them in her hair. (*Laughs to herself*) Tasha looked in the mirror and laughed and said "Mommy I think I got too many ribbons in my hair", and I said "no baby Mommy just likes to see you in red. It's my favourite colour." (*2 beats*)

I want to believe that you tried to love me, but I just couldn't feel it. I couldn't compete with Sandy. Because I lost that race before I even started. And I've been trying all my life to win it, just to get you to love me; not as much as you loved Sandy, but just a little bit. And now you're dead. (*beat*)

I know I'm supposed to feel something. Maybe cry, maybe mourn. I want to feel something. And for God's sake, you're my mother and you're dead and I want to cry and I can't. (*2 beats*) (*Tries to convince herself*) Maybe at the funeral I'll cry. Because I'm wearing a black dress, a black hat, black shoes, black stockings – all black. All black. Mom I'm wearing all black! Mom could you just look at me, I'm wearing all black! Please will you just look at me? I'm wearing black (*3 beats*) I've been wearing black all my life.

i remember

(excerpt from the one womban show *stuck*)

NAH-EE-LAH/NAILA BELVETT

when my reality changed
when perception began to alter
how i saw those around me
and unknowingly began to construct
new philosophies
that would prohibit me
from playing in innocence
when friendship making
became a viable networking tool
and dinners were served in soup kitchens
cause community work looks good on resumes

soon thereafter the in crowd became the out crowd
and the once out crowd became the cool crowd
cause now there were critically analyzing all the other crowds
when wearing brand names and labels
meant you were consumed by commercialism
no longer signs of fashion but those of selling out
when having money wasn't cool
cause it meant you subscribed to the system

who would have thought – well definitely not our parents
that being poor would become a badge of honour
exchanging second hand store shopping finds
when permed hair meant processed and fake
so it had to be wrong and not just a hair style
when kinky nappy natural hair
suddenly elevated me to conscious sistah clout

i remember
when we smiled at police officers
and thought they'd save us from the bad guys
until we realized that in their minds that meant
our borthers, fathers, uncles, cousins and
even aunt gloria's cute son jamal
and so we branded those uniformed
beasts, 5-0, pigs, upholding fascism
convinced they were only there
to serve and protect
and break a brothas neck
we decided we were wiser
with a better understanding of the 'system'
changed first names to something more african sounding
johnny became ade kunle zimbabwe
and everyone bought into consiousness
maybe they sold it at convenience stores
with pendants, copper bracelets
dashikies, egyptian musk incense and more
when everyone became an 'artist'
cause it meant you could create
find ways to articulate anger and hate
form poetic rhymes/rhythms
plucking on people's heart strings
twist turn and cultivate words
into shock value form – legitimize hate
masquerade it, package it and compartmentalize it
into word spoken abstract intellectual prose that lies
cause poetically you can be "conscious"
and still say nigga and call anyone a devil or a swine

chastize, mock or criticize
legalize it with poetic justice
and the audience will clap and fall in line
now i never talk to my once four best friends
last i heard
suzy was a married single mother raising their three kids
suzette was pregnant with a baby father on permanent pregnancy leave from
her
ann-kari was telemarketing part-time finishing her degree in political
science
don't have to be a rocket scientist to know she ain't gonna get paid with
that
johnny, sorry ade kunle zimbabwe, i heard he's a mechanic at canadian tire
and me too – i'm canadian and tired
of living in this cold place
on the outside and on peoples' insides
feeling like a stranger in my birth place

now i've adopted a jamaican patwa
in just these last few years
clutching on to any semblance of heritage
wishing i could adopt that sweet immigrant language of "back home"
romanticizing the freedom of back home
ungrateful wondering why my parents ever left home

now it seems
i remember too much
from history books read over the last few years
it seems
i remember too much
from critical analyses around pot luck dinners and sunday midday brunches
it seems
i remember too much
from lectures and workshops and conversations with new friends
it seems
i remember too much
from reasonings with sisterins and bredrins,
muslims and christians

bald heads and rastas
now it seems
i remember too much
to continue to live in peaceful numb in babylon
some might say i remember too much

Dirty Laundry

(Excerpt from *My Upside Down Black Face*)

JAEL EALEY

The following is comprised of Act I, scene I and Act II, scene I. The conversation is between Lela, the main character a light-complexioned black woman adopted by white parents, and Cathleen, a 30-something white woman that approaches her in a Laundromat.

A Laundromat in Toronto. Lights rise on two women, Lela and Cathleen, folding and sorting laundry.

CATHLEEN: Excuse me. I'm so sorry to bother you, but if you don't mind my asking; what do you use in your hair?

LELA: I'm sorry?

CATHLEEN: My daughter. She has hair just like yours and I was wondering what you use in it. I can't seem to get it under control. Do you get it done around here?

LELA: I go to an Italian hairdresser in Brampton. That's where I'm from, so I just go to the hairdresser when I go home.

CATHLEEN: Really?

LELA: Yeah. I've been going there for years. I don't know...I've been to some black hairdressers. They've got really good ones around here. Did you want to perm it?

CATHLEEN: Oh no! I want it natural. Like yours. I love the way yours looks. So soft...Kara's is the same. I just wish I could get that kind of curl in mine. What kind of products did you say you used?

LELA: I don't know...sometimes nothing...sometimes...

CATHLEEN: Really?

LELA: Sometimes I don't have time. But usually I use Italian stuff too: Joy-ko...Kanra...gels, but not the heavy kind...

CATHLEEN: Wow, so you said...(gets a piece of paper and pen from her purse)...Joy-ko...Kan-ra...and these are gels?

LELA: Yeah...well they're...they're gels, yeah. (Lela continues sorting her laundry)

CATHLEEN: Because I've been using this...hair goop...I can't remember the name of it...uuhh...B...it begins with a "B"...anyway, I've been using that on Kara – that's my daughter– but...I can't remember the name of it. Anyway, a friend of mine recommended this hair goop—her daughter has the same hair too and she uses it on hers. I find it sort of makes her curls stick together. It's harder to comb the next day, but I don't know what else to use. I've tried a bunch of different products. They have that one section in Shopper's. Well, I usually go to Hy and Zel's. It's so much cheaper there...dollars difference on pretty much everything. They have the same thing at both, but I can't seem to find anything that works for Kara–

LELA: I'm sure the Italian products will work. They're lighter.

CATHLEEN: Thank you so much. I'll try that. Are you mixed?

LELA: No.

CATHLEEN: Really, how did you luck out with such beautiful hair?

LELA: I don't know.

CATHLEEN: Does anyone else in your family have hair like yours? Because it's quite unique and very soft. *(Reaches out and grabs Lela's hair)*

LELA: *(pulls away)* I'm sorry...I'm...I'm just going to make a phone call. It was nice talking to you. *(Searching for phone in purse)*

CATHLEEN: You too...actually, while you're here, I was wondering if you could help me with another thing. I'm looking to get my hair in dreadlocks. Do you know a place that does them?

LELA: No. Sorry. I've never had dreads.

CATHLEEN: I think they look so elegant and my hair grows back really quickly, so if it didn't work out or look right I could just cut them. I just want to do something different and I just think they are absolutely stunning.

LELA: Okay.

CATHLEEN: My husband's mother used to have them. She passed on about a year ago.

LELA: Yeah...well...I don't know anywhere you could get them done. Sorry I can't help you.

CATHLEEN: Do you come in here often? Because, there's this black woman that comes here with two little boys, she has dreadlocks, and I wanted to ask her about them because I want mine just like that. Do you think she does them herself?

LELA: I don't know.

CATHLEEN: You said you went to some of the black hairdressers around here, did you ever see someone getting them done? Maybe I should go ask, eh? There's one at the end of this plaza.

LELA: Maybe you should. Maybe you should go.

CATHLEEN: I'm sorry?

LELA: I'm just not really understanding why...why you want to get locks?

CATHLEEN: Well, I don't know. I just want to do something different with my hair. We're going to Jamaica to visit family and I don't want to have to worry about doing it.

LELA: *(muttering under her breath)* I can't believe this...

CATHLEEN: Sorry?

LELA: Forget it.

CATHLEEN: Did I upset you?

LELA: Just forget it, okay.

CATHLEEN: I don't...?

LELA: I don't think you should get locks. I wouldn't...and I don't think the store down the street or any store in downtown Toronto, or anywhere else for that matter, should let you get locks. That's all.

CATHLEEN: Excuse me?

LELA: Locks. I don't think you should get locks. I don't think you should get them.

CATHLEEN: Look, I'm sorry I asked.

LELA: You should be. You should be down right embarrassed.

CATHLEEN: I beg your pardon...

LELA: I don't think you have a clue what you are asking about. I don't think you realize...anything...Your husband, your daughter...You just don't get it!

CATHLEEN: What does my husband have to do with any of this?

LELA: Exactly.

CATHLEEN: What, are dreads supposed to be a 'black thing', now?

LELA: Yes, they are actually, but you don't care about that do you, you just want to believe that you have the right to do anything.

CATHLEEN: And you're telling me I don't.

LELA: I can't believe you. I can't believe that you would be so bold...that you would do something so politically loaded without even thinking about what it possibly meant to people...your mother-in-law.

CATHLEEN: What are you talking about?

LELA: I'm talking about Bob Marley. I'm talking about your husband's mother and the woman that comes in here with her two kids. I'm talking about people who have been through things that you have no clue about...

CATHLEEN: It's a hairstyle. And I'm pretty sure there's no racial claim on it as being either black or white. Or anything else for that matter.

LELA: Of course not. This is a free country. It's certainly okay for you to do whatever you want, whenever you want. Just so you know, marrying a black guy does not make you a hero—it doesn't give you the license to adopt his culture and his history as your own. It doesn't make you some ultra-liberal, open-minded, white wonder poster child.

CATHLEEN: Okay, that's enough. You disgust me–you and your racist attitude. I don't claim to be a hero or a poster child, but I face the same stuff you do out there.

LELA: Are you kidding me? Are you for real?

CATHLEEN: ...I face it every time I hold my husband's hand, subtle as it may be. Because the fact is there are people like you everywhere. Obsessed with what other people are doing with their lives. Obsessed with issues that need to be buried. Need to be forgotten. There are some things I want my daughter to learn about history and the past. And there are other things I hope she never has to learn.

LELA: Because it will make you feel better, right? Fine. Puff up her hair, dread yours. See how screwed up she gets when she realizes the world just isn't the way her dear mother tried to paint it. You may be able to choose your battles, but you can't stop what she learns on her own, trust me. She'll figure it out eventually. She'll figure out what you did and she'll blame you.

CATHLEEN: Well, we'll just have to hope people like you don't affect her as much as...

LELA: Give me a break.

CATHLEEN: When I see my husband...my daughter...I see them just like I see everyone else. I see them just the same. I love them just the same. I don't see them or you or anyone else as different. I see them the same as I see everyone else in my family. I see everyone the same.

LELA: And that's supposed to be a compliment?

Lights fade on the women sorting and folding their laundry.

MALE. Black. Age 21-25

(Excerpt from *My Upside Down Black Face*)

JAEL EALEY

Monologues addressing the representation of race in film and television appear throughout the play. The following monologue appears in Act II, scene V.

Every audition I go to is pretty much the same thing. I go across town to some run down audition studio to play Jermaine or Jackson and I say two lines, you know "Ooooh girl, you looking good...mmm-mmm" or "Oh, man! Your moms made you wear that? *(laughs and poses for a shot)*" and then I go. I come back home and I wait. And I wait. I see the same guys every audition. It's me, this big guy—and this guy is diesel—so he usually gets the parts, you know, as a bodyguard or a bouncer in a club—those type of things. Then there's Chris—we all just call him "C"—he's got the whole hip-hop-baller-look down pat. The two of us usually hang out and laugh at the lines they throw at us. You can tell they're written by white people. *(Imitating)* "Yo dawg, that girl was fly, man." It cracks us up. There's a few other guys that float in and out too—mostly pretty boys. We call them the Four Tops. They just come for the "star quarterback" calls or the shaving commercials. Look how fresh and clean we look. Those guys give us pure jokes. It must take them hours to get ready. I literally get up, shower, and I'm off—15 minutes, and most of that's spent picking my outfit. These guys pluck their eyebrows, line their goatees. You know straight pretty boy styles...and sometimes they get the part. Sometimes they don't. So why do I need to butter myself up like that? It's too much work.

I just went to this audition the other day. And all of the same guys were there. Cee, the Bodyguard, the 4 Tops and myself—all of us waiting around to audition for – that's right "Jamal"*(quoting)* "A streetwise basketball star who dreams of making it big in the NBA to support his family". We're all sitting there, reading these lines thinking...'Do I really want this part?' And for the most part, I think we all do. I'm sure we could all use the money. And trust me, it's some sweet change.

I'm a musician. I got in this to get in front of the camera and get seen doing my thing. Then I can do what I really want to do. I've been working the other angles and it's just not happening. So I could really use the money. But what am I willing to do to get it?

So I got up. I got up and left. I'm not playing no b-ball jamming, street slinging thug with a strung out mom and an absentee father. I'm not playing that anymore. I just left.

Cee called me later on. He left too. They all did, even the Four Tops. That woman came out to call for the next audition and no one was there. I'm sure they found someone though. They always do.

Lights fade.

My Upside-Down Black Face

(Excerpt from *My Upside Down Face*)

JAEL EALEY

The following excerpt is from Act II, scene VI and features Lela, a 20-something black woman, adopted at a young age by a white family. Raised in a predominantly white Toronto suburb, Lela moves away from home to attend art school downtown. In the final scene of the play, Lela reveals her thoughts and addresses the audience directly.

LELA: How can I be with someone who doesn't see me...who I see as something terrible? I don't feel we're ever at the same place. And how can I stay with someone that makes me feel like that. I feel privileged...I feel privileged, like...and maybe this is a bad example...but I feel like a house slave instead of a field slave. And I'd rather be a field slave than have to be grateful...or feel grateful for some "privilege"...

I don't feel beautiful. I don't feel entirely beautiful with Marty. I feel privileged. And I want to be beautiful, not because I'm black or unique-looking. I just want to be beautiful. I want beauty to be me.

I know what you're thinking, and I'm not crazy and I'm not confused. You want to believe that, but I'm not. The last year has turned me upside down. But I'd rather be upside down than what I was before. I was comfortable before. And as soon as I became comfortable with who I thought I was I realized that's exactly how you want me to feel. And there's no reason why I should be. There's no reason why I should be comfortable. Listen to me. Listen to me. LISTEN TO ME...Listen to me....Just listen to me...if you could just LISTEN. I want to tell you that I'm not crazy and I'm not confused. I want to tell you that the last year has turned me upside down. But I'd rather be upside down than what I was before. Comfortable. And as soon as I became comfortable with who I thought I was I realized that's exactly how you want me to feel. And there's no reason why I should be. Because I'd rather be a field slave than a house slave and have to feel grateful for some privilege.

You think black. You think dark. You say a well or a corner or evil or bad. You say black. And then you call me black. You turn around and call me black. And then I'm black and I'm nothing. I'm that whole—that nothing-ness. That empty place. And I'm angry. I walk around angry. I think about it. I see it. I feel it. I want to talk. I want to be angry and don't you stop me. You have no right to say anything. I'm not going to let you say anything. I'm just going to tell you you can't say anything so you can see how it feels to be me. To be pent up with opinions and angers and frustrations and not have a chance to feel better by getting them out. I see them. They're in there. You have things to say to me. You want to hate me or you want to hug me. But I won't let you. I won't let you feel better. Because that's exactly what you want. And I want beauty to be me.

Lot.1975

(Excerpt from *Lot.1975*)

WEYNI MENGESHA

The following is an excerpt from Lot.1975, which Weyni Mengesha was commisioned to write, and is the first play ever produced by Up From the Roots. It was written in response to notion that black people do not go to theatre. The show played to a sold out audience of 600. The following scene opens the play. The Senior Monitor, a mayoral figure, is addressing a group of young people on their pledge day. These scenes follow Fitzgerald, Asia and Duane, members of Lot.1975.

Act 1 Scene 1

OPENING

While audience lights are still on pre-show music is turned off. Man enters audience in his pajamas and sits in a seat in the middle of the audience. He puts his hands down his pants and points a T.V. remote towards a huge screen at the front of the stage. He presses the button on the remote, the audience lights go out, and an image is projected onto the screen. We see channels being flipped until we arrive at the Senior Monitor's televised address.

On Screen

SENIOR MONITOR: Citizens. Young ladies and gentlemen of LOT.1975. I am very proud to be here as your country's Senior Monitor, only two weeks away from the year 2000 Annual Pathway Day. It has been years since my 25th birthday, but I still remember that exciting time in my life. Embarking on a journey where I would meet my destiny, and become one of the many important pillars that make up our society. It is now the beginning of the new millennium, and we are looking to you, Lot.1975, to make us proud. It is time to pledge a party discipline, and contribute to the growth of our society. Today you will hear three speeches from the leaders of the life-fate parties: the Spirits, Intellects and Assets. Listen carefully to what they say, because the choices you make today, are the foundation for our future. Without further adieu I would like to give the floor to our first speaker, the leader of the Intellects Party, Dr. L. Monroe.

(End of excerpt from Scene 1. *All the party leaders give their addresses and The Senior Monitor closes with his best wishes to Lot.1975)*

Scene 2
*(Scene jumps between three areas: 1. Fitz's Kitchen 2. Asia's Kitchen
3. Duane's living room)*

Fitz's Kitchen

MRS. MORTEMER: Come to breakfast Fitz.

FITZ: *(screaming)* I said I'm coming!

MRS. MORTEMER: (*to MR. MORTEMER*) Jeffrey you see me trying right?!

MR. MORTEMER: I know honey, it is going to take time and patience to change things around here. Remember what Dr. Chapmen said, "Don't give in to Negative attention".

MRS. MORTEMER: But I CAN'T TAKE NOT KNOWING...

FITZ enters the room

FITZ: Not knowing what?

MR. MORTEMER: Sit down son.

MS. MORTEMER: I'm making your favorite, peaches and cream pancakes.

FITZ: Mom I thought you said cereal. I don't got time for all that. I gotta jet.

MR. MORTEMER: Son, your mother wanted to surprise you. Where do you have to "jet" to so badly?! I thought your last exam was going to be held at *12:00 on Thursday (voice overlap)*

Asia's Kitchen

MS. WOODS: *12:00 on Thursdays*, Saturdays and Sundays you're coming with me to help with the church food drives.

ASIA: Mom I have basketball league on Thursdays.

MS. WOODS: Well I have to work every day. Do you see me complaining? NO. I understand it's about sacrifices. The Lord says give to others more than you desire for yourself. When are you going to learn not to be selfish? It's always about you playing basketball in those little shorts. If you spent half the time in the scriptures that you spend in those shorts, you might prepare yourself for your Spirit's pledge. Personally, I think your lustful desires could block your chances of getting in.

ASIA: Lustful desires?

MS. WOODS: All my friends are coming back to me after watching your games saying how healthy you look and how beautiful you look. Healthy?! Why aren't they telling me about your jump shot?

ASIA: Nobody says that.

MS. WOODS: Yeah? So why did Father Phillip come over here last night concerned about the effect you might be having on the young boys.

ASIA: (*under breath*) - because Father Phillip is a pervert.

MS. WOODS: What did you say! Don't get smart with me Asia. Father Phillip is a spiritual leader. Don't think I don't see you. Every time a man treats me well *you get upset. (Voice overlap)*

Duane's Living Room

MR. RIGHT: *You get upset!*

DUANE: Dad, I was 8 when I cried in *Bambi.*

MR. RIGHT: You were 8, but you were 15 when you cried in *Stand by Me.* Boy when I was 8, I was slitting the throats of livestock with my dad! And you were squirming under my arm just watching a cartoon deer getting offed!

DUANE: That's a lot different Dad.

MR. RIGHT: Of course it's different. Back then, little boys acted like men. Now little boys act like little girls. It's your 25th year son. I never thought it would come but here it is, and if you want to join the Assets you got to be tough. (*Puts his foot on the table*)

Duane: Dad, why do you always have to put your feet on the table?

MR. RIGHT: Good Lord (*says to heaven*) it's like you never left Beth. You got your son running around like Benson, telling me what to do.

DUANE: I just don't see the logic in messing up a perfectly good table.

MR. R: I don't see the logic in being your biological father, but I don't question everything. (*Duane rolls his eyes*) I'm just joking boy where's your sense of humor? Anyway, you need to start with the lawn, so stop hiding your head in those love songs you're always writing. This is the real world son; I got *to tell you (overlap)*

Fitzs' Kitchen

FITZ: *...to tell you*, Supa and me were thinking of running for volunteer positions at the law firm.

MR. MORTEMER: That's great son! What position were you thinking of?

FITZ: Well, we were going to go and see what we like, and..uhmm .. what is left.. and all that. Anyways, I was wondering if you could spot me some cash from that government bonus you got. I got to get some nice clothes, you know, to make me stand out, so I can get this job.

MR. MORTEMER: well Fitz remember what we said about unplanned expenses...

FITZ: I know Dad, but couldn't we make an exception since this could mean a really good reference? I mean that could be just the push I need to make it into the Intellects.

MRS. M: Fitzgerald (*excited*), does this mean you're going to write the entrance exam for the Intellect party?

FITZ: Uhmm... yeah. I'm seriously thinking about it.

MR. MORTEMER: That is great son. I will put fifty dollars in your account this afternoon.

FITZ: Thanks dad. I'm out.

MRS.MORTEMER: Fitz your...

FITZ: Mom put some pancakes in the fridge for me, alright. *(Fitz takes off)*

MRS. MORTEMER: Jeffery, I don't know why we spend so much money on the psychiatrist when the problem is simply you.

MR. MORTEMER: Beverly, do you expect me to put a minor roadblock like money in his way to joining our party? He is Intellect material. He just needs to apply himself.

MRS. MORTEMER: When are you going to get it Jeffrey? When you're broke? Hmm? He has no intentions of joining the Intellects. He wants to be an Asset! Yesterday Kunle's mother offered me his tutor's number because she heard how Fitz is failing.

MR.MORTEMER: But that Is ridiculous. His professor said he is a prime Intellect prospect, and that he could do the exam with his eyes closed.

MRS. MORTEMER: He can Jeffrey, he has been telling Kunle and who knows who else that he can't. Jeffrey, he does not want to join the party. Maybe you're pushing him too much, maybe that's why...

MR. MORTEMER: (*Cuts her off*) look Beverly, my family have been Intellects for generations. It is more important for me that Fitzgerald keeps the tradition.

MRS. MORTEMER: You listen here Jeffrey Mortemer! I might be the first Intellect in my family, but that doesn't make me any better than my parents who were the hardest working Assets in this city.

MR. MORTEMER: (*desperately*) Look, I didn't mean..I just don't want to give up on him...

MRS. MORTEMER: (*cuts him off*) *Your priorities are obviously different than mine!!! (overlap)*

MRS. MORTEMER exits

Duane's Living Room

DUANE: *Your priorities are obviously different then mine.*

MR. RIGHT: How do you figure?

DUANE: I don't think being tough should be involved in getting you to a higher level of life.

MR. RIGHT: Look Duane, life is hard. It doesn't work with you. If you don't stay strong it'll push you down.

DUANE: I believe in strength dad, but I think it comes from believing that you're weak...

MR. RIGHT: Oh no Beth, here it comes.

DUANE: ...belief that you're just a weak vessel in the hands of the Superior Spiritual Power will make you strong in your faith, and thus a confident and strong person.

MR. RIGHT: It's not healthy to be stuck on one idea. Your mom spent her whole life slaving in the Spirits Party and look where that got her. Rest your soul Beth.

DUANE: Dad, it was Mom's time to go. Like you said, this life doesn't work with you, that's because it is not pure. Evil lives here, but it can't survive in the after life. So when one is pure, they are moved to a pure and peaceful place.

MR. RIGHT: That's what you're betting on?

DUANE: That is what my heart knows.
MR. RIGHT: Well, that's your problem. You need to start thinking with your head!

MR. RIGHT exits

<u>*Asia's Kitchen*</u>

MS. WOODS: You need to start thinking with your head, Asia. Young men have urges that are chemical, therefore, urges they're unable to control. Young ladies wearing revealing outfits are asking to be prey for all those raging hormones out there.
ASIA: Mom, I'm just saying women have beautiful bodies. Were we given these curves to be covered?
MS. WOODS: I used to have a body like yours you know *(pauses and smiles at her memory)*. Every boy in my school used to beg me for a dance just to put there hands on these hips. Of course back then I was the best dancer in the school. Everyone knew I invented the "Tandigroove" *(laughing to herself as she starts the move)*
ASIA: Mom...
MS. WOODS: *(still in a smiling thought)* yeah...
ASIA: Yeah, hi, we were talking about the dangers of raging hormones.
MS. W: *(snaps back)* Yes, look Asia, if they were not powerful, your father would still be around. If it weren't for Father Phillip introducing me to the Spirits I would have... I don't want to think about it. But you have to think about it, think about how I was saved and how you can be too Asia! Child you know how my hypertension gets *(sits herself down)*.
ASIA: Mom, I believe I was sent here for a reason. Look at your bad health and my gift for science, you think that's just a coincidence? I want to help you and others like you. Mom, I scored the highest science mark in the province. Doesn't that tell you something?
MS. W: Yes, it tells me that the Ultimate has blessed you with intelligence, but that does not mean you should join the Intellects. It gives you more reason to dedicate your life to him, thanking him.
ASIA: But what if I can learn to heal through science, the Lord would work through me. Wouldn't he?
MS. W: *(she exits leaving Asia alone at the table)*. You see Asia that is the problem with all this new-school-talking, tearing you from the Lord, calculating and experimenting, trying to add...You can't add to the beginning, it is before all things....Oh my Lord, LOT.1975, what is to come of this generation?

DANCE

"Now that hip-hop is so mainstream and many mistake 'booty shaking' for hip-hop dance, I try even harder to go back to the basics and make a positive statement through urban dance."
–Asha Tomlinson

Black Magic, University of Windsor Sports Weekend, 2001

Steps Toward an Afrocentric Dance Scene
ASHA TOMLINSON

Five, six, seven, eight... The girls mark through their dance over and over again.   Grim expressions are painted on their faces, their brows scrunched up with worry.   Their minds are working overtime thinking of the many steps, waves, jumps and turns they're about to perform in just a few minutes. Stomachs turn with butterflies, palms are sweaty; the mood is TENSE.   Only one minute left. The girls gather round, they hold hands and pray.   Then, it's show time.   The stage door opens. The girls run out from left wing. Suddenly those frowns turn into smiles and their heads bop and weave to the upbeat hip-hop tempo.   Bodies move and bounce to the rhythmic beat in ultimate synchronization.   There's no barrier between the music and its dancers. They become one on stage.   The energy soars through the crowd transforming into cheers and clapping.   The girls dance off stage feeling as if they just left another planet.

Expression through dance — there's nothing like it.   The art form prevails throughout the eras; black people have pioneered many dance styles from slavery right through to what urban dance is today. While many people are aware of Caribbean, African, and American influence on dance, what about Canada's influence on the art form?   Better yet, what about Toronto's influence?   Although, we are one of the most diverse cities in the country, are we bringing African, Caribbean and hip-hop dance to the mainstream?   Do we have leaders in the field leaving long-lasting legacies?   The answer in short is both yes and no. Toronto is "hip" to the dance scene and there are many pioneers, but there is a long way to go.   We are making our mark slowly but surely.   It's up to future generations to keep the various dance styles alive.

Keeping Traditions Alive

Patrick Parsons is a member of the black community who has successfully brought Afro-Caribbean dance to the forefront. Some consider him to be the Alvin Ailey of Canada. Parsons is the founder and Artistic Director of Ballet Creole, a school and company dedicated to showcasing Afrocentric dance.   He describes his work as a revitalization of traditional dancing (from the African Diaspora) combined with Canadian aesthetics.   When Parsons came to Canada in the early 1990's, touring with the Toronto Dance Theatre, he quickly recognized the need to express more of his culture through his dancing.   There were no black professional dance theatres that provided this outlet so Parsons decided to carve his own niche.

"It just opened my eyes.   I was able to see more and that made me want to do more.   I've always been into African spirituality and that drove me to find my inner roots," says Parsons.   And so the Ballet Creole School of the Performing Arts was born.   It started with just one class but has catapulted into numerous classes, a professional school and dance company.   Ballet Creole has received some accolades, Parsons says, but it's been a long haul.

"My main focus for this institute is to have it become internationally known as a school that presents dancers of Alvin Ailey calibre and [people] don't have to go to the U.S. to get it."

Parsons comes from a very artistic family, rich in Trinidadian culture. His mother was a dancer. His father played pan and both grandmothers were singers. The arts were all around him, from a very early age.

"I was being groomed for this [all my life]. I wasn't picked by anyone in particular but from the energies, I just followed through," he says. "The griot is one who holds a certain amount of history and passes it on. Now I'm training and influencing others through song and dance."

There is yet little awareness in the black community about what Afro-Caribbean art is doing for Canada. Parsons adds: "[We must] share what we know. Giving and sharing is not losing, no one exploits you but yourself. Everything comes back around full circle."

Hip to the Hop

From Africa to the streets of the Bronx — hip-hop planted its baby roots when break dancing emerged in the 1970s as a popular mode of expression. It was created as an alternative to gangs and other negativity. Then it rocked the world as millions of young people embraced it. Groups like Rock Steady Crew and New York City Breakers took the old school dancing to the next level. Out of break dancing, new school hip-hop was formed, a more choreographed style of dance.

Break dancing was a big influence on Fabian Evelyn, the creator of the well-known MonsterFest hip-hop competitions.

"Watching Turbo in the movie *'Breaking'* when he was dancing with the broom – that really set off my love for dance," he says.

Evelyn performed break dancing at school shows, but realized there was no formal platform for dance teams to showcase their talent. So, he created his own platform. He organized the first ever MonsterFest hip-hop competition in 1999 and it was a hit. The ball started rolling from there.

"I became hungry for exposing dance talent and people were interested in seeing more of it. It shows young people can put something positive together without causing trouble."

According to Evelyn, MonsterFest gives dance teams something to work towards and raises the profile of urban dance because it was at rock bottom in Toronto in 1999.

"Hip-hop is very popular now with artists like Sean Paul using dancers in his music videos. Now even the Americans are showcasing Canadian talent," says Evelyn.

The Rise of Booty Shaking

Unfortunately, sex sells and we are seeing more and more videos with less hip-hop dancing and more 'booty shaking.' For example, hip-hop artist Q-Tip released several music videos filled with women shaking their 'thangs' in front of the camera. Many of the women wore five-inch heels, miniscule shorts and skimpy tops.

"These videos are a sad reality," says Tanya Andrews, Artistic Director of urban hip hop dance troop, Black Magic.

"What kids see on television is very powerful. There's a difference between tasteful and tasteless dancing," she says. "Kids think what those video girls are doing is cool." That is why it is important to have dance groups in Toronto that present the other side of hip-hop dance.

There are currently thirteen female members of Black Magic and, "[they] always make sure to come up with tasteful choreography. [They are] bringing the art back to its true form." Thanks to homegrown talent like Shawn Desman and U.S. artists such as Missy Elliot, hip-hop dance is coming back around.

"It's all about evolution too," Andrews says. What makes Toronto's urban dance scene so unique is its multiculturalism. Black Magic has members of many ethnic backgrounds and "our choreography is a fusion of many cultures. We're creating our own form of dance combining Flamenco, Indian, and African dance styles into our hip-hop routines," says Andrews.

Passing on the tradition while North America is cashing in on the misogynistic sexual images of hip-hop dance, Cory Daniel, a.k.a Benzo, from the break dance group Bag of Trix is taking hip-hop back to the basics. He focuses on the international scene because people in Asia and Africa still appreciate the old school styles. What's even more important is that B-boys and B-girls are now becoming mothers and fathers and can pass on the positive tradition. "Especially in Toronto, we're one of the first generations to pass this [art form] on. Now that I have kids, it's my duty to keep the tradition alive."

Dance is about feelings, expression and telling a story. It represents freedom, creativity and strength. Once such knowledge is shared and passed along, it will be on the shoulders of future generations to keep the art form a strong and positive force.

LYRICS

Kamau

Introduction to Lyrics

Can you hear it? The streetcar screeching to a halt, the school yard seagulls swooping down for a noontime meal of garbage. Beginning with the methodical rhythm of the heart, Africans have always produced music. Removed from Mother Africa, the music of black Toronto attempts to define us and legitimize our presence in a city wherein our citizenship is often questioned. Whether it is Maestro Fresh Wes discussing the colour of Canadian dollar bills in 1989 or Kardinal Offishall educating the airwaves about Toronto's colloquialisms, music carries important stories of our time, our culture and our people. While hip-hop has exploded into a mega million dollar industry, it becomes apparent that societal fortification is second place to danceable beats and frivolous lyrics. However, emcees and songwriters such as K-OS and Solitair still maximize the medium to challenge complacency and encourage their listeners to consider alternative views on issues.

Toronto-based musical artists in hip-hop, R&B and reggae benefit greatly from black owned Flow 93.5 FM, Canada's first commercial 'Urban' radio station, on the air since 2001. One can hear songs from Saukrates, Choclair, Blessed or Melanie Durant at any time of day. However, campus/community radio plays a significant role in disseminating the music of artists not backed by commercial interests. "Project Bounce" on 89.5 FM now produces thirty-five hours per week of hip-hop programming. As new avenues for expression through music open to black artists, so must the commitment to authentic stories of African-Canadian culture.

T-Dot: "It Ain't Where You're From, It's Where You're At"
DEL F. COWIE

"We don't say you know what I'm sayin'/ T-dot says ya dun' know"
-Kardinal Offishall from "Bakardi Slang", Firestarter Vol. 1: Quest For Fire (Universal, 2001)

When I first heard Kardinal Offishall rhyming these words, I couldn't help but stop and smile. I was at the video shoot for the song, trying to track down emcee Tara Chase -- a member of one of Toronto's premier hip-hop crews the Circle -- for an interview. When I walked in she was initially nowhere to be found, but Kardinal Offishall -- perhaps the most recognizable member of this crew -- definitely was. Surrounded by lights and cameras at the back of the nightclub set, Kardinal performed seemingly endless takes of "Bakardi Slang". All I knew about the song before I showed up to the shoot was its title and was curious to know what it was about, but as soon as Kardinal started rhyming it all became clear.

At first it seemed like an ingenious take on Big L's 'Ebonics'. The late Harlem, New York rapper had lined up meanings in so-called proper language in the song and proceeded to provide his own definition, translated in specifically black New York slang that he branded 'Ebonics'. While the set-up of the rhymes in the Big L song are influential in the structure of Bakardi slang, it is just one of the influences on the song. Through Kardinal Offishall's own inimitable delivery, the song was peppered with Jamaican patois. The song's production, provided by fellow Circle member Solitair, is a dancehall-infused riddim replete with explosive effects that are usually heard coming from reggae sound systems.

Yet the song represented more than a mere convergence of sounds and ideas from African-American and Caribbean cultures. While Toronto-born Kardinal Offishall hails from a Jamaican background, he takes care to indicate the song is very specific to Toronto's West Indian population as a whole, not just Jamaicans: *You think we all Jamaican, when nuff man are Trinis, Bajans, Grenadians, and a whole heap of Haitians/Guyanese and all of the West Indies combinedT/o make the T-dot O-dot, one of a kind*

By doing this he expands the song beyond its African-American and West Indian influences and localizes it to the city of Toronto. More accurately, Bakardi Slang is referring to a place or space known as the T-dot. Although the words, phrases and meanings used in the song weren't foreign to hip-hop heads in Toronto, it was the first time there was an attempt to articulate them in such a specific way for an audience inside and outside of the city. In this way, the song becomes far more significant than the sum of its beats and rhymes. It represents the marking out of a space and territory that draws on and is dependent on a number of different influences to facilitate its identity. But this space did not appear out of a vacuum. A statement as specific as "Bakardi Slang" couldn't have been made unless the elements already existed. The construction of the T-dot has become more specific and refined over time in Toronto hip-hop and its existence allows a space for artists to express themselves that references the past present and the future.

Now if your from Uptown, Brooklyn- bound,
The Bronx, Queens, or Long Island Sound,
Even other states come right and exact,
It ain't where you're from, it's where you're at

--Rakim, from Eric B. & Rakim's "I Know You Got Soul", Paid In Full (4th & Broadway,1987)

The importance of territory cannot be underestimated in hip-hop culture. In the late eighties, the California city Compton became synonymous with the incendiary hip-hop of NWA. In the nineties, Atlanta became known as the "Dirty South" and Philadelphia, once a major hip-hop centre in the eighties, reinvigorated itself and became known as "Illadelph." The redubbing of these cities coincided with fertile creative periods and recognition for hip-hop acts from those cities. In New York, as hip-hop culture emerged in the late seventies and early eighties, the claiming of space was so rigid and insular, identification was based on what borough you were from, as Rakim succinctly outlines. You couldn't simply just be from New York City. As hip-hop culture spread throughout the country and the entire world as a global phenomenon, new scenes sprouted. With rap artists claiming regional space, these cities began to transmit their own experiences and realities.

Toronto's relative proximity to New York however meant that this act of self-definition was not an automatic event and has taken a while to develop. As in many other Canadian cultural arenas, the influence of the United States was great. Much of the hip-hop that found its way to Toronto was broadcast on Ron Nelson's pioneering CKLN radio show "Fantastic Voyage" on CKLN (88.1 FM in Toronto). The radio show precipitated a demand for prominent New York hip-hop artists to appear at Nelson's Monster Jams at the Concert Hall in Toronto. The link between Toronto and New York extended to tapes being sent to Toronto from New York by family members and the efforts of many Toronto residents to pick up hip-hop and R&B music broadcasting from Buffalo, NY radio station WBLK despite its weak signal. Pioneering Canadian hip-hop acts such as Maestro Fresh Wes and Michie Mee had to negotiate this complex terrain when they emerged in the late eighties, when hip-hop from New York still had a virtual stranglehold on the direction of the culture. To put it into context, West Coast hip-hop was only beginning to get begrudging respect and few hip-hop acts had emerged from the South; it certainly wasn't 'dirty' yet.

Maestro Fresh Wes' single 'Let Your Backbone Slide' from *Symphony In Effect* (LMR, 1989) was Canada's first bonafide hip-hop hit single. On this record, Maestro identified himself within a number of differing spaces: *But like I said before, I'm not American/It's who you are, not the way you went/We all originate from the same descent*

Not only did Maestro indirectly affirm his Canadian status by denying he was American, he betrayed the influence of New York hip-hop as he seemed to reference Rakim's phrase "it ain't where you're from it's where you're at." While the first two lines illustrated a tension between Canada and the United States, he proceeded to make a thinly-veiled reference to Africa. Though he displayed Diasporic tendencies that tied together black experiences over geographic distances, he was often intensely local in his outlook in his recording catalogue. Maestro's Scarborough stomping grounds are often mentioned in his rhymes. On 'Conductin' Thangs' from his second album *Black Tie Affair* (LMR, 1991), he refers to coming "from Birchmount, just north of Glendower" and that his rhymes are "attracting more brothers than Kennedy station" over a ska-influenced beat.

West Indian musical influences however, were more prominent in the music of Michie Mee. She effortlessly incorporated dancehall reggae into her brand of hip-hop and changed her flow and voice into Jamaican patois from New York influenced rhyme patterns at a moment's notice. The change in her lyrical style was often underscored by a change in the music from funky soul breaks to a dancehall riddim, a style that won her the respect and an affiliation with KRS-One's influential Boogie Down Productions crew. As the very first Canadian hip-hop artist to be signed to a major label deal in the United States along with her DJ LA Luv, she released the album *Jamaican Funk - Canadian Style* (Priority, 1991). The title alone, much like Maestro Fresh Wes' lyrics, pointed to national and diasporic concerns at the same time. The title track further heightened this reality by assertively stating repeatedly "I'm a Jamaican!" While residing in Toronto, at the same time, Michie Mee definitively identified with her heritage.

Another Toronto hip-hop act that explored this realm after the pioneering of Maestro and Michie were the Dream Warriors. Influenced by the Daisy Age era initiated (and later ditched) by Long Island, New York group De La Soul, the duo of King Lou and Capital Q brought an abstract and quirky approach on their *And Now The Legacy Begins* album (4th & Broadway, 1991). However, while Maestro and Michie consciously marked out geographic regions, the Dream Warriors' abstract and esoteric approach meant these issues were rarely explicitly addressed in King Lou's lyrics. Ironically, this lack of specificity may have contributed to the group's appeal to a wider audience as they became popular in Europe and achieved some success in the United States. The Dream Warriors' eclectic approach to music that drew on plenty of jazz influences also tapped into reggae as their single 'Ludi' demonstrated. King Lou made the Diasporic link by recalling a family game tradition with his mother and later extended it by shouting out several West Indian islands.

Clearly, the same affinity for diasporic traits that appear in the music of Maestro Fresh Wes, Michie Mee and the Dream Warriors are evident in Kardinal Offishall's "Bakardi Slang" and have long been a part of Toronto hip-hop. But it is apparent that the T-dot Kardinal Offishall references is a much more specific environment than these artists. So what precipitated the change to a more local outlook?

The commercial faltering of Canadian hip-hop in the early nineties must have surely played a part. When he released his sophomore album *Black Tie Affair* (LMR, 1991), Maestro Fresh Wes was played on significantly less radio stations than when he first emerged with "Let Your Backbone Slide". The album was still a relative success, but discouraged by lack of support from the Canadian music industry, Maestro soon left Toronto and moved to New York where he released his third album *Naaah, Dis Kid Can't Be From Canada?!!* (Attic, 1994). While Maestro, Michie Mee and the Dream Warriors continued to record and release music, they could not retain their profiles and replicate their earlier successes at this time and few viable hip-hop acts were being nurtured or developed by the music industry.

Faced with this situation, emerging Toronto hip-hop artists began to look to their immediate surroundings and negotiate their artistic voices within a local context. In doing so, they effectively were re-drawing their boundaries. With access to outlets such as commercial radio and major label contracts virtually sealed off, Toronto hip-hop artists began to set up independent record labels as a means for their voices to be heard. Labels such as Groove-A-Lot, Black Employed, Blueprint, Knowledge of Self and Kneedeep began issuing material. Ghetto Concept was perhaps the first group to emerge out of this second wave of Toronto hip-hop on tracks like "Certified" and "E-Z On the Motion", and their seamless mix of West Indian and American influences on these tracks pointed to an increased assurance. Other artists such as, Thrust, Da Grassroots, Frankenstein and Circle members Kardinal, Choclair, Saukrates among many others began to emerge releasing 12" singles.

Community radio was the primary place to hear these records. While Ron Nelson's "Fantastic Voyage" show morphed into DJ X's "The Power Move" and remained the city's most important hip-hop radio show. CIUT 89.5 FM's "The Masterplan," co-hosted by Toronto emcee Motion, and CHRY 105.5FM which had a number of hip-hop shows were also spaces where Toronto hip-hop artists could reach a local audience. Additionally, regular events like the freestyle haven Planet Mars, the multidisciplinary creative arts program Fresh Arts, and Phemphat's all-female Honey Jam showcases also represented spaces where hip-hop artists could hone their craft.

While many national outlets were not receptive to hip-hop music, an important exception was video. Through Videofact, a program funded by MuchMusic, independent artists could gain nationwide exposure through the airing of their videos on the national station. Through this outlet, artists could fashion a visual identity for themselves and many Toronto emcees took advantage of this. In a video co-directed by then little-known music video auteur Little X, Choclair's "What Does It Take" was an example of Toronto hip-hop artists increasingly claiming their space. Filmed on location at Toronto Island it clearly frames the CN Tower, Toronto's most recognizable building in the background. Choclair was arguably also one of the first emcees to utter the phrase "T-dot O-dot" on wax on his "Just A Second (Remix)". The live shows of many Toronto hip-hop artists, particularly the Circle, helped to popularize the term that quickly came to be known simply as 'T-dot'. While Kardinal Offishall is a member of this crew, Kardinal himself has actually credited K-4CE, a pioneering emcee in Toronto's hip-hop history who collaborated with Maestro Fresh Wes, as the person who originated the phrase T-dot.

Ironically, while Toronto hip-hop artists had shifted their focus from a national to a local context, it was the national overtones of "Northern Touch" a posse cut single from Vancouver B.C. crew the Rascalz that proved to be a catalyst for widespread recognition of independent Toronto hip-hop. While it formed an East-West alliance with the Rascalz and Checkmate hailing from Vancouver (a.k.a. Van City) and T-dot rhymers Choclair, Kardinal Offishall and Thrust, the crossover success of the single strengthened the local identities of these artists making them increasingly difficult for the Canadian music industry to ignore. Choclair was soon signed to Virgin Canada, marking the end of a long period of domestic major label indifference towards Toronto hip-hop. Eventually, Kardinal Offishall and Thrust would also receive major label deals. The significance of Choclair releasing *Ice Cold* at the end of 1999 was not lost on Toronto's independent hip-hop artists as many artists such as Mathematik, Citizen Kane, Monolith and Nefarius began releasing more material, making important contributions to Toronto's hip-hop canon.

While Choclair's signing was symbolically important, Kardinal's release of "Bakardi Slang" in the spring of 2001 also represented a significant moment for Toronto hip-hop. It marked the convergence of a song with specifically local references made by an artist on a major label that was aided in its popularity by the presence of a newly launched urban radio format in the form of Flow 93.5. Before this time, there were certainly no urban radio stations or major label contracts to be had. In effect, it was a watershed moment. It represented the culmination of the T-dot's independent hip-hop development over the years and its changing relation to space. From this position it was possible for Kardinal Offishall to form a link with premier dancehall DJ Bounty Killer on the 'refix' of "Bakardi Slang". The fact that Kardinal was able to do this and also join forces with Jamaican-born New York emcee Busta Rhymes on the remix to his next single "Ol' Time Killin" indicated the diasporic call in his music was being answered. While Canadian hip-hop artists had a long standing history of collaborating with American hip-hop artists and having West Indian influences in their music, these collaborations in particular positioned Kardinal as a central Toronto hip-hop artist and have helped to raise the T-dot's profile within a global hip-hop context.

However, Kardinal Offishall is just one of countless Toronto hip-hop emcees grabbing the mic and plying his or her trade through rhyme. While "Bakardi Slang" remains an important recording and is a song that has come to represent T-dot hip-hop to many outside of the city, there are artists and hip-hop afficianados in the T-dot that it may or may not represent. As the T-dot has become more identifiable over the years, from the days the city's most prominent emcees referred to themselves within a national construct to the current specific outlook, it is evident the framework and breadth of the T-dot will continue to change as more voices join the fray. They will articulate their experience and may even, like Scarborough crew IRS, create their own 'T-dot anthems'. New voices will bring new experiences, new lyrics, new flows, new deliveries into the mix, advancing the hip-hop art form. These emcees may casually throw out the term T-dot for crowd response or to simply state where they're from, but when they do, something is happening at a deeper level. By invoking the T-dot, they unwittingly or consciously refer to everything that has come before them, yet at the same time, they have established a space for themselves, and are setting the stage for their own story to be told.

H2O
WAKEFIELD BREWSTER

There once was a time when we flowed like rhyme
Ebbs and tides lived on our insides
We took no free rides
Just rode waves and dug sacred graves
'Cause we knew the earth saves

And when we took to our knees
To drink at our sea's shores
Eventually we ended up creating sea sores

As we gazed into the depths
And only saw the surface
The face of folly to come

We drank our own reflections with gluttonous vanity
Gulped down gallons with thirsty profanity
Draining drops like three-pointers
Pollute den shoot into the earth a dirty needle
Da sewers beneath are the burning veins of acid rains
Hydrants erupt like popping zits
Sludge and sickness pumped through pipes
Walkerton walked in medical plights
It blacked out some lights den led to court fights

And while da poor fight for it
Da rich wanna whore it
We will make you pay!
We will make you pay!
Da flow of H2O we goin' keep on da stay —
Locked up!
Dey ain't gonna die for their supply be locked up

Damn your creation of the Canal Suez
And neglectful flex on da Exxon Valdez

Oil and water – dey just don't mix
But slicks in puddles give kids head tricks
Dey think that it looks pretty
See all the colours?
Now they can finally
Touch a rainbow
And make it dance
Like a beautiful woman

But once again the image of life is washed, washed away
Back to murky and muddy waters
Our oceans sing da blues
Environmental channels hype to bring da bad news
Dat we all gonna lose
I'm getting too confused

'Cause I started to drink my water from a bottle
For da vehicle of pollution was chokin' on da throttle
Den a rumour went about dat I just could not believe
I spelled Evian backwards and found I was naïve
My gut is on da grieve
Believe you me I'm in 'nuff pain 'G'

I first thought I'd contracted ileitis or colitis
But from da water cooler I drank gastro enteritis
See how Mother Nature spite us?

She did it
She done it
She'll do it once again
Fool us into thinking we can cheat our fated end
For we put the pain in her rain
And showered her with disrespect
And we gonna thirst worse before we get our lives in check

'Cause when the oceans all evaporate
We can't make juice from concentrate
No fluid moving up and down in the locks
No creamy whipped potatoes from a cardboard box

We are damned and doom ourselves a drunken dry demise
In da stretchin' of da skin and da bulgin' of da eyes
'Cause nobody tries
We'd rather drink lies

For we hold fast to da mistakes of da past
Latched to da ludicrous and not liquid life

'Cause we can't let go
Forget what you know
We've forgotten how to flow

Like water

Life Sentence
For the mothers and the brothers

MOTION

Prelude:
Mummy's keeping vigil at night
Counting the seconds till the key turns in the lock and she can finally get rest
Felt the pain in her chest
The very second that the bullet went to tear his vest
"Soon come, Mummy" he said when he left the rest
Never again return to the warmth of her breast...

Verse:
My blocks are mystic
Stars and statistics
Ladies pushin' babies
That could end up in body bags
Maybe 'cause of red and blue rags
Or a kid in a doo-rag
Maybe some beast who think you got a
Piece up in your school bag

Swear he never knew that
Your child was just an average kid
Never held a pound of steel in his life
Maybe this chick who got a knife
He said she's tryna give him jacket*
In a fix at 16, she's crazy stressed
And wouldn't have it
Or it's the wrong place and time
On the block with just a dime
Cop takes him to the line
Say point your finger
You can trade some other nigga for your crime
Boy, you still do the time
Catch a shank in the back
Waiting on the phone line...
Couldn't hear when Granny talk about signs
She's dreaming dreams
Talking 'bout you losing teeth
And still you went to the jam
And since your boy's boy owes somebody else a grand
You take a shot for your man's man
That's the end to all your Mom's grand plan
That started when she pushed you in the baby pram
Now she's the last to zip the bag
Before they put it in the coroner's van...
Blocks are mystic
Stars and stats
Mothers dreaming of destiny
Wishing they could guarantee
Your life without the tragedy

Hoping and praying their kisses will be enough
To save their baby boys
Before life gets rough

---

*He said she's claiming he's the father of the child

Unclean Lips

DWAYNE SEWELL

Chorus:
I am a man of unclean lips and my people are losing their soul
I am a man of unclean lips while my people are losing their soul

And I say, how shall I speak to my people?
How will they know that you sent me, God?
How shall I speak to my people?
And how will they know that you sent me?
I am a man of unclean lips while my people are losing their soul

Verse:
Who am I that I should go and tell Mas' Pharaoh let my people go?
Yet you tell me to keep on walking and while I'm talking it's you that they'll know
For I will be your mouth piece fi chat and spit out peace, a doctrine of love and of truth
Now some will fall on good ground, while some just fall down and will never bear fruit
The time is near don't lay-lay fast and pray say Father please forgive me
For I accept your son and when him come down all will fall on their knees

But who am I that I should tell you what you should do, when I need help?
Who am I that I should tell you what you should do when I need help too.

I am a man of unclean lips and my people are losing their soul.
I am a man of unclean lips while my people are losing their soul.

The Black Man Struggle

PECULIAR I

Tribute to his Excellency the Right Honorable Marcus Mosiah Garvey

The Black Man struggle is a rough kinda struggle, yuh nuh. The Black Man struggle is a kinda struggle weh very funny. Yuh haffi mek di best use of a situation although yuh nah have nuh money, yuh nuh. The Black Man struggle is a kinda struggle weh dread but it even dreada when yuh wear all the covenant pan yuh head, yuh nah see it.

The Black Man struggle as a youth, inna dis time yeah, is like an endangered specie, and I find I self within that circle of such an endangered specie. And I nah feel safe Rasta, yuh nah see it. Chant men down . Fire! Fire man! Fire man!

> *"Griotism is a license to kill bigotry, oppression, selfishness and hate. Armed with a pen as pistol and the instinct of a sniper during a blackout the griot licks the light of truth and spits bullet-like words that penetrate the darkness to find his/her nebulous target."*
>
> **– Seth-Adrian Harris, Poetic Filmmaker**

Come fling di fire, come fling lightening and earthquake fire, cramp and paralyzing fire fi bun out di wicked fire, fire, fire because how come you a go tell I seh that this is a world of democracy? How come you a go tell I seh that these are no more days of slavery. Well I say all these are just modern hypocrisies.

This chant a come straight from the heart of hearts, yuh nuh. Ah hope the I dem can bide up this one yah. Nah feel no way a so wi talk. The Black Man struggle is a rough kinda struggle. The Black Man struggle as a yout' is kinda cute. When yuh strive fi speak the truth and to live upright, then I hear Marcus Garvey speak who was merely born abused, insult, humiliation, whose fore-parents can only be compared to the prophet Job, as likewise lifted his bowed head and raised it up to God's skies and cried:

"I am a man and demand a man's chance and a man's treatment in this world"

Such is the Black Man's struggle, yuh nuh. Such is the Black Man's struggle, yeah. The Black Man struggle, yuh nuh. The Black Man struggle, yeah. The Black Man struggle is kinda full of what, psychological brutality, not to mention physical brutality from Babylon and their fallacies.

The Black Man struggle is a kinda struggle weh, yuh have all yuh family, yuh nuh. And is like yuh not even have them, yuh nuh see it, because what – Babylon stand as what, a separating force mek yuh feel like yuh pickney dem is not even yuh pickney dem and like all way yuh nah worth nuttin, yuh see it. Because what – the standards on which Babylon is built, worked and respected is merely on vanity.

But as I say, the man who seek of vanity and hath no love for i-manity shall fade away, a so Jah seh. Run come seek love, man. Let love find thee. Fire a bun inna Babylon dis a di Black Man struggle from a young Black Man's perspective. Don't make I look as if I am savage. I have heart of flesh, I have blood coursing tru these veins. I have a mind to think I have a tongue to speak. I have energies to block this little chant.

Selassie I live man. Hold strong lahd, hold strong. Now go and teach the youths in the way in which they ought to grow and they will nevah go astray. Rastafari see and know it's individual trials and universal judgment.

The Black Man struggle is a rough kinda struggle. Dis yah struggle is like yuh have so much energy both physically and spiritually. And is like what, yuh energies dem become internalized and then yuh feel all a way. Yuh feel like yuh a fight against all yuself, yuh nuh. Is like certain forces just come in pan yuh as if dem wan mash yuh dung.

The Black Man struggle mi a deal wit, yuh nuh from a young Black Man's perspective. It is like an endangered specie. And I find I self within such circle and Babylon dem drive a lot a fear inna I and I. Dem keep I and I in bondage and subjugation, degradation that when I and I try fi mek all a likkle move inna progressive way according to Babylon and their rules. Is like what, the whole world shut slam all dem doors pan yuh, yuh nah see it. And then what, yuh feel all a way. Yuh feel like yuh not even belong but really and truly I and I nuh belong inna dem yah lan yah because I and I have a home. But dese tings happen to I because I and I are far away from I and I home.

Yuh cannot be inna strange land and expect not to be treated as a stranger. Strange philosophies, strange culture. When I try fi hold I likkle sanity is like the whole world gone crazy. All I have, all that I have, is this likkle chant. Now tell I what more, what more do you want, eh? All I have is this likkle chant, tell I what more, what more do you want than I hear Garvey speak who was born abused, insult, humiliation, whose fore-parents can only be compared to the prophet Job, as likewise lifted his bowed head and raised it up to God's skies and cried:

"I am a man and demand a man's chance and a man's treatment in this world"

Such is the Black Man struggle, yuh nuh. Such is the Black Woman struggle. Such is a people's struggle. A crucial kinda struggle that more time yuh haffi all sit een and call down the archangels dem from Zion fi come and accompany, yuh nuh. Because, these people round and about I is nothing but wah – repellence, they aren't attractive. They are nothing but repellence, repelling, repelling, repellence. oh Jah, give I deliverance!

POETRY

Al St. Louis, Urban Boulevard, 2003

Introduction to Poetry

Toronto is alive with poets. Inspiration comes in gusts of wind on the subway tracks, traffic on highway 401, broken campaign promises and political correctness. These streets remember the revolutionary words of dub poets Michael St. George, Clifton Joseph, Lillian Allen and Devon Haughton. Their rhythm takes flight in a new generation of speakers who use poetry to deliver philosophical medicine. While open stages abound, many spoken word artists are producing showcases throughout the city. Up From the Roots and the West Side Cipher mix poetry with other media, while Toronto Poets sticks to one art form.

For the most part, the black poet continues to share her work in the familiarity of African-Canadian circles, whereas blacks are only marginally present at the often stuffy mainstream literary readings. Alternative spaces are necessary in order to develop the art in environments accepting of innovation. Our work is a marriage of substance and style, favouring the conscious over the cryptic. For such storytellers art is not a luxury, but a necessity giving birth to initiatives like fiwi aat space, When Words are Spoken, The Pitbull Reading Series and La Parole.

A Trip to the Underground

CHRISTINE THOMPSON

I hop on the train
Running late
Forgot to wear glasses
Can't see map
Going northbound
Move closer...
Still can't see
Destination

Eyes catch sight of little girl
Cute little girl
Dark, charcoal-coloured, cute little girl
Thick girl
Hiding her face from me behind her even thicker mother
A modern day Grandma Moses
Tubman
Is no man
Woman
Feeding her son from breasts
Liquid manna
Able to feed nations other than her own
As well as her own
Trying to get it to its destination
Getting it to its destination
Heading northbound

Beautiful
Natural
Solemn woman
Expression speaks louder than her voice
Speaks of heartache
Break up
Unemployment
Unpaid bills

Mouths to feed
No time to sleep

No real words come, but low hum
Like Negro spiritual
Like blues
Like jazz
Like a call to respond

Her blessing – being strong
Her curse – having to be strong all the time
Just trying to get her children home
Heading northbound
My stop is called
Think to tell her she's my next poem
But change my mind
Don't think she'd really care
Just trying to get her children home

Now
Emerging from Underground Railroad
I know I'll never be the same

Heroes
AL ST.LOUIS

Mine eyes have seen the glory of the coming of the Lord
In one accord they'd sing, as song bells ring and rang they sang
Far past the legal drinking hour
Praying for "Showers of Blessings" and "Pennies from Heaven"
Each one teaching the other what it means or meant to be a true soprano
They'd hit high notes and harmonize
With eyes to the skies fixed on the prize
Staring straight through the stucco

Just as the little wood boy would or could or did stare at Gepetto his maker
Their Creator the Heavenly Father, the Great I AM
And I am thankful
More like grateful and humbled that their faith was greater than my own
And this was known and shown that in those times life was rough
Tougher than the toughest tough
But their songs thundered with the deepest bellows
As they sang with visions of meadows and greener pastures
Praying
"The Lord is my shepherd, I shall not want. He maketh me to lie down in green pastures. He leadeth me beside the still waters."
Then chant songs like, *"When the Roll is Called Up Yonder"*
And boisterously yell out "FREEDOM!!"
Because they were not yet free
You may shake your head and disagree, but if you think about it neither are we
Times have not changed
Faces have, places have, but the game is still the game is still the game
They had one vision and their collective mission was to change the world
For, in the pearl of each eye life's oceans raged with fire
That no water could quench or douse or put out for that matter
But what really mattered was the matter at hand
And knowing that the hand that rocks the cradle is the hand that rules the world
They clasped hands and prayed for access to the crib
Some felt that violence was the key and had vision of gaining control
"By any means necessary"
Others felt that peaceful or passive resistance was the road to travel
Or march for a better choice of words
But still collectively they knew what they wanted
Regardless of how the enemy taunted and haunted
Like the devil in the blue dress, like the devil in the blue dress
Were they faced with stress; yes
Were they battered and beaten; yes
Were they misused and abused, treated like their existence was of non-existence; yes
And were they slain and hung from Oak trees like strange fruit?
Yes they were yes they did yes they do
But where two or more are gathered, there the Creator is in the midst
And while some drew fists, others marched on
Singing spiritual songs "Free at last, Free at last"

Knowing that the goal was clear they continued to strive on without any fear
So today I pay homage to the real heroes of the war
The black men and black women who died in order for our race to endure
Malcolm, Martin, Marcus Mosiah Garvey, Harriet Tubman and the underground railroad
The countless others unnamed and faceless
Hungry for freedom yet settling for nothing less
I pay homage to you
I honour you
I thank you for what you have gone through
I thank you for who you have allowed me to become
Because now in the bright rays of the sun I can see that I am a man
I can open my eyes and ingest the light
I can stand tall and stand strong for what I believe is right
Yes, mine eyes have seen the glory of the coming of the Lord

> *"To paraphrase Peter Tosh, the term griot represents word, sound and power for me. A griot is a manifestation of those terms."*
> – Kevin Reigh, Co-founder Tallawa Arts Project

E' Cyan Bun Dung*

MEL WHITE

Gimme di bass
Gimme di drum
Gimme dat
Mek mi gwaan and galang (repeat)

No matta whey mi go
No matta whey mi run
No matta whey mi come from
E' cyan bun dung!

Gimme dat
Mek mi gwaan and galang (repeat)

Dem tek whey mi name
An' dem tek mi cultcha
Kill mi mudda an' rape mi sista

Chain up mi fahdda an' hang mi bredda
But mi nah guh no whey
A yah so mi dey
Mi fulla gumption
An' mi fulla black pow'a

Wedda mi brown
Or wedda mi black
Wedda in a Englan' or in a America
In a Africa or in a Canada
Wedda pan top or under attack
No matta whey mi dey
A di same sin' ting

Mel White

Gimme di bass
Gimme di drum
Gimme dat
Mek mi gwaan and galang (repeat)

Mi bredda gone a jail
Di woman dem a wail
Mi sista dem a breed
An' mi people dem a bleed
But mi a gwaan same way
Fa dey is no damn way
Mi a go back dung now (repeat)

Gimme di bass
Gimme di drum
Gimme dat
Mek mi gwaan and galang (repeat)
No matta whey mi go
No matta whey me run
No matta whey mi come from
E' cyan bun dung!

---

*It can't burn down

Black Beautiful Me

JAICYEA HAMILTON-SMITH

Black Beautiful Me
Black Beautiful Me
How happy and special I am to be
Black Beautiful Me

My lips so full
My hair so thick
Every time I comb it I have to use a pick

My beautiful brown eyes see so many things
Some make me smile
Some make me cry
My caramel skin so soft
So smooth just like within me
Black Beautiful Me

"We are a hybrid of all kinds of experiences, but above all residing in Toronto, you know you're black and you're proud of it."
– Nadia L. Hohn, Co-ordinator, Iced in Black Film Festival

Jaicyea Hamilton-Smith, La Parole, 2003

The Story of My Life

KAREN RICHARDSON

It's the story of my life
Walking
Talking
Tripping on my feet
While people stand up gawking
Experiences rocking my thinking find
God was always there
It really blows my mind
So if you care to listen
It won't take much time
But that's just the story of my life

I'm not from the ghetto. So please let go any pre-judgment you had. I didn't grow up in a hood where you earned your stripes by being bad. I was blessed to meet my family. When the struggles were real. Born with a spoon in my mouth. Stainless steel.

My mother stayed at home until I was nine. Raising two boys and a girl, while weekdays would find my father taking courses and working two jobs to inspire his young ones with vision. One day they'd be having, not just wishing. Reaching home when we were sleeping to eat leftover callaloo that Mom was dishing.

In those days there were no gunshots, no sirens and no electric fence. But there were relatives who hoped that they could clear up the suspense surrounding this land of opportunity that tells black students the classroom isn't for us all. New aunts and uncles left their island home to live with us in Canada each fall.

Times were tough, but Ma and Pops believed that they could work together to give their kin a fighting chance to make their own lives better.

Unfettered by stats that say that blacks are likely to live lives of crime, my folks instilled teaching in us that stands the test of time. Hooked-on-Phonics came along long after we had got the picture. Instead we read our first sentences from the pages of scripture. In retrospect my parents must be glad they took to heart "Train up a child in the way he should go, and when he is old he'll not depart."

It's the story of my life
Walking
Talking
Tripping on my feet
While people stand up gawking
Experiences rocking my thinking find
That God was always there
It really blows mind
So if you care to listen it won't take much time
But that's just the story of my life

I was just a little girl, but I can still remember moving way out to the west-end before my brother's birth the next September. To a spot where the main road was still covered in dirt. Our family didn't come to visit and I know that hurt my Mom. She never dreamed she would feel so alone. Just because they chose a home they could afford to own.

In our new working class community, white was the rule. I learned new words like "Nigger" out on the field at school. Suburban life became the only thing I know. White kids try to take my life with mounds of snow. Black boys laugh in class. The other girls all had straight hair. Black girls saying "she acts white" cause I liked school and didn't care if I fit in.
Maybe I didn't. Maybe we didn't at all. But as a family blessed by God we always stood tall through financial sacrifices and the same old song: falsely accused by teachers 'cause he said / she said always proved us wrong.

My parents fought through these and other trials to see their children go far. By example, they instilled in us just who we are. Staying together, though the times and stats may not agree. They freed their minds from popular opinions of what black immigrants should be.

It's a story of two people born in poverty who rose above expectations on their lives by recognizing love had lifted them up from the struggles of their youth. And if they could not give their children money, they could always give us truth.

So judge me if I'm disturbing your monolithic black concept. Keep your melting pot and give me freshly tossed salad. These types of black experiences are equally valid. Out of reverence to God, ours was a home filled with love many families lack. And though we're not from the ghetto, we are no less black.

It's the story of my life
Walking
Talking
Tripping on my feet
While people stand up gawking
Experiences rocking my thinking find
God is always there
It really blows my mind
So if you care to listen it never takes much time
But that's just the story of my life

Christmas Eve In Jane & Finch

SETH-ADRIAN HARRIS

I skip across the storyboards of my life
In search of a picture of Jane & Finch on Christmas Eve
A picture that doesn't say
"You got what I could afford
Cause Christmas is too damn close
To the end of the month, baby"

I wanna paint a picture
That's kinda like the birth
Of baby Jesus
Maybe we'll have a woman named Jane
Give birth to a bird in the ghetto
Yah! That's it
Then we'll have three brothers
Come by with all the party favourites
And an open eye
To make sure
Baby birdie
Isn't his

Christmas Eve in the projects
The labyrinth
Of misguided connections
Under the umbrella
Of some holiday love

Swallow your pride and take that gift
Swallow your pride and give that gift
We all poor
Ain't no mystery in that

Crack the bottle
Drop the needle
Let's have some fun

It's all for the kids
We all know that Christmas Eve
In Jane & Finch

I got the skates

Loadstone

SETH-ADRIAN HARRIS

If the history of humankind
Is of migration
Then the stories
Of my greatest grandmother
And
My greatest grandfather
Are transfixed in a rock of immortality
That was discovered by pure accident

Time in
Time out
Times time before
The bodies of immigrants
Were placed in pine boxes
And buried in a land light years away
From the place of their birth
But
One
Was buried with a loadstone
And this made all the difference

She unclasped her necklace
With a loadstone pendent
A loadstone
That was found by her grandfather
While he and other Japanese men
Blasted through the belly of mountains
In the Rockies
Bridging the borders
With serpentine steel

She fastened the necklace around his
Black
Cold

> "*[Living in Toronto] I realized the experiences I went through living in New York, Chicago, L.A. and Detroit are global.*"
> – Ernest Carter, Poet, Visual Artist

And still neck
Closed her eyes to the calm of blackness
And remembered the words of the Negro blacksmith
From Chatham
Who shaped and refined the loadstone
Into a pendant
She remembered him saying
"You'll attract more questions than answers
With this pendant but don't you worry
Questions are quests and in life you can ask
For nothing less."
She became pregnant with those words
And for the first time she knew he was gone!

She closed his casket
And it was lowered
Down!
Past the bowed heads of his three children
Taiko
Lyric
And Jembe
Down!
Past winding roots
That pointed to his place of
Eternal intermission

Eternal intermission!

Eternal!
As his soul that is
Smooth
Spherical
And slight
As the head of a sperm

Intermission!
As in
The magnetic force of the loadstone

That attracts his soul
Pulling him closer to the
Centre of attraction
Then
BAM!
He is through the other side
Gently floating up
Higher
Mingling with the night air
Ascending
Higher and higher
That he could see without eyes
That the stars are pinholes in heaven's drapes
With a light that calms as it calls
"Come home"
"Come home"
And with every calling
He is pushed forth faster
And faster
As if he were pure light
Buoyant on a beam
Streaming from the bedrock of his being

He gently drifted through a hole in the black drape of night
And embraced the energy of his
Mother's Mother's Mother's Mother's Mother's Mother's Mother's
Mother's Mother's Mother's Mother's Mother's Mother's Mother's
Mother's Mother's Mother's Mother's Mother's Mother's Mother's
Heavenly Father's
Mother

And as his spirit
Melded with her miraculous power
Vestige visuals of his future-present appeared like vapor from the invisible

He saw his great granddaughter Sheniel
As she hid her shoes among the mango trees
So she would not have to go to school

He saw his great great grandson Caleb
Dip his hand in the sands of the Valley of Pharaohs
And pour it into an hourglass

He saw his great great great granddaughter Mieko
On the Great Wall of China selling shirts that read
"Japanese-Jamaican-Canadians do it better"

He saw his great great great great grandson Malaise
Looking at his dirt lawn in Jamaica
Wishing that he could pull the rain from the clouds
Down
To
The
Ground
To prove that where there is mercy
There is life

He saw his great great great great great granddaughter Desdemona
Sitting under a Maple Leaf tree
Looking up towards the sun
Which made the leaves look like tinsel
As they glittered and reflected the light
That gave them life

He saw his great great great great great great grandson Phinius
On the snow banks of an outdoor ice rink
Trying to squeeze size five feet in size four ice skates

He saw all this and more
And as the images came
He became more and more
United

With the great force that is his ancestry
So much so that within a stellar wink
All that was left
Was the luminous outline of a smile

That faded as fast as it formed
Leaving only the sensation of a message
Of which I'll share with you:

What you see
Is an astral projection
From the perception
Of my mother's mother
On the flipside of time

I speak to you in tongues of her making
And make no mistake
I speak to you
May angels huddle
Around your beds and whisper
All of God's secrets
And may your soul be
Guided high and travel far
By
The
Loadstone

> **"The griot has the daunting and rewarding task of bearing and revealing the knowledge, experiences, wise tales, wisdom, histories, and languages of the Afrikan (sic) peoples."**
> **– Malik I.M., Poet, Radio Host CKLN 88.1**

My Husband
NANA YEABOAA

We lived in the village of Assesewa
We married after my bragro*
Babies they didn't come
The oracles had said
Two you shall get
Later they will come
In the days of the white man's first visit
I had my children

Egya Kofi came
From the white man's house
He came
Around him we gathered
He told tales of a visit
A visit to the white man's land far and beyond
To see his world
All were proud of him

II

Egya Kofi came with a white woman for a wife
His lawful wife he said
He signed papers and she was given to him
Hmm, just a piece of paper for a wife?
He built a mansion away from the hut were we lived
In the white man's language they spoke
A sister I was presumed to be

I cook but he eats not
He says when I cook it's all dirt
I have not what the white woman uses
He complains when he eats my food
He says I overcook

Nana Yeboaa, La Parole, 2003

When the moon blesses at night
My husband comes to me
But my husband complains
He tells me I am dirty when he feels the shea butter on my skin
He says I smell like a shea butter factory

He says my hair is too thick
He can't run his hands through them
My husband says that the flesh of my skin is fat
My breasts too big
And my buttocks too much
He says I am too dark

When my husband comes to me on nights when he is denied
Hear him again! He says I am too rigid
I do not wiggle and giggle
That is why he doesn't want to make love to me

My husband says I am too backward
Because I use herbs
I am my own doctor
I have remedy for headaches
I have remedy for worm infestation
I have remedy for malaria
Remedy for impotence and bareness
All these are in the forest

III
I till the land from dawn to dusk
The merciless sun beating on my back
The rains soothing and balming
The rewards of my hard work
Cattle, sheep, goats and chicken
All he knows is kill and eat with his white wife

To my house he points
The fruits of my labour are directed
To a wife who is my rival
Bought by a piece of paper!
One who does not toil with her hands
But paints them
Those shall be dinner
Servant I am not
The sultry taste of sweat
Produces food

My husband has turned into a hypocrite
My husband says a woman is not to talk back to her husband
But I see his white wife raising her hand to him
I am a woman too, a mother of his children
A woman who cooked

A woman who washed
And warmed his bed
Gave him a pillow of breast
Now he doesn't like me because I am black

IV

In the old days you were a proud man
You had the most beautiful woman
My hips were the jealousy of your friends
My eyes the emerald of light
The smoothest skin like polished stone
You adorned me with cowries, beads and gold
Now you distinguish between colours
Because I am black you like me no more
Two babies and the oranges are still strong
They stand with no support
These you say are not ideal
The little ones you cannot hold
The bones that grind against you
That you love

V

Through rain and shine
Thin and thick
I was the star that led protected and comforted you
In my bosom you found solace
Lovers we have been
Friends we were
I was a mother who breastfed you
A sister who chided you
Now I am no good
To you an educated man
A fool lost in the world of his ancestors

Bragro is a ceremonial rite of passage before Akan girls attain 'womanhood'. The Akans are the largest ethnic group in Ghana. The Akans speak different dialects of Twi. They can be found in the southern and eastern part of Ghana.

A Tribute to Film

NADIA L. HOHN

If a picture is worth a thousand words, the value of moving images must be infinite. Since the 1970's and 1980's black filmmakers from all over the T dot have been making films about issues affecting our communities. This practice of filmmaking among blacks in Toronto began with films by Caribbean immigrants such as Jennifer Hodge Da Silva, Claire Prieto and Roger Mc Tair. The first African Canadian feature films emerged in the 1990's from the creative minds of Clement Virgo and Stephen Williams. Young directors including Charles Officer, Dawn Wilkinson and David Sutherland continue the tradition. The poem below is a tribute to Toronto's griots in film. Italicized words refer to titles of African Canadian films.

Life in Toronto wasn't easy
For the black folks already here
Never mind the newcomers—
Police brutality, racism,
Community violence, poverty,
Out of Africa*—
These became the yokes

> **"I want people to read this and say 'I didn't know there were so many Black Canadian filmmakers.' This is our work these are our stories."**
> — Nadia L. Hohn, Co-ordinator, Iced in Black Film Festival

A rhythm bubbled
Under the pavement
Surged through the concrete
And the steel
Buzzed through the highways, suburbs, the inner city
This sexy, creative energy,
I began to feel

The city became a new landscape
For many artists who were *Coming to Voice*
To find their place.
But *When Morning Came*
Our *Rude* attitudes
Made us

Soul Survivors
Who were *Speaking for our Dead*

Though our *Journey for Justice* often led us *Home to Buxton*
And sometimes to *Another Planet*
We were just searching for *A Way Out*

*italics reflect titles of films by Toronto fimmakers

We didn't have to look too far
For in our *Father's Hands*
We were so full of *Thanksgiving*
Within me, I found a *Girl Who [Said] Yes*
To fulfilling my *Destiny*

My Brothers in the Music helped me sing a Short Hymn
And though it was Silent
The War within me continued
That Instant, I Dreaded what I might find
As I became *The Last Witness to this Dreamscape*
But it was *A Long Time Comin'*
As I waited to sing my *Song of Freedom*
And *Save My Lost Nigga' Soul*

In my youth I picked *Dandelions*
Played with *Maple* keys
And through the years

The Style of My Soul
Began to emerge and
The *Love Came Down*

> **"I don't believe in African-Canadians, I believe we are AfriKans (sic) living in foreign reserves, in this case Toronto; thus, I write from the "Nomad" perspective: telling stories of the AfriKan (sic) experience in the Diaspora, and singing songs about longing for home."**
>
> **– Yannick Marshall, poet**

Africa Wailin
AFUA COOPER

Stereo-Prophet trow down
at Bathurst and Bloor
an di dj bawl out
"yes, crowd a people
mi seh mi love unu*"

An wi trow some stones on the boys and girls
who throw we resumes in the garbage bin

An seh "we've hired already"
while di media report that in we hood
is 60% unemployment

Africa wailin
as Stereo-Prophet trow down
inna downtown
at *Tequila*˝
and 300 sing as one
sing along wid the dj
sing along wid the singers
wid Sanchez an June Lodge
and Gregory, Tony Rebel,
Cocotea, Beres, Sizzla,
Beenie Man and Delroy
and Garnett Silk

Hello Mama Africa
How are you?
I'm feeling fine and I hope you're fine too
and Africa wailin
Alas, alas Kongo
nari, nari Kongo

Africa wailin
as Toronto get hot
and Black people dance
communally
heads up
backs arched
eyes watchin
a far away scene
hands boxin
di air
and feet and hips move
inna kumina, nyahbinghi
300 dance as one

and woman wid dem man rent
a tile
and di man wid di hangle conneck
wid di triangle
and di dj leap in di air
a Watusi dancer
as fire fire
from the Spear
lick him inna him head
and him grab a second mike
hold both a dem a him mouth
and start fi talk in tongues

nari, nari Kongo
alas, alas Kongo

Woman in weave, red, gold, and green
dread wid locks down to dem feet
we all hold hands as we embark
on a journey
as we cross di passage
wid Freddie inna big ship
and Marcia is troddin us to Mt. Zion
for a healin and baptism

And we help each other as we begin dis passage
weak and tattered
cold and afraid
Lady Saw is embarkin as Oshun
Burning Spear, di griot from Kangaba
Rita an exiled priestess from Kumasi
will start a new world religion
and we love each other
we gentle wid each other
as we continue di journey

An Africa still wailin
and we still crossin
no jobs here in Babylon
is jus pure botherayshan
our men led like sheep into prison
and ours sons lost in whiteness

Africa still wailin
for her children
scattered on white shores
wanderin in di trangle
tryin to find their way home

Woman in red, green, and gold weave
and dread wid locks down to their feet
women in shiny shiny clothes
tight like rass
an men in basic black
wid gold chain allick
confess their love to each other
as we sing wid the dj
and the singers
songs etched in our memory
songs that live
at the tip of our tongue
and we hold hands and begin a journey
tru a narrow passage
as Stereo-Prophet trow down
inna downtown
and two beas' car park pon di street
watchin I n I
Ready fi caas shackles pon we again
an as wi fling rockstone inna Babylon
boone
Africa is still bloodclaat wailin

wailin
wailin
wailin

Dr. Afua Cooper, La Parole, 2003

*unu - Jamaican term for 'you'
**Tequila Lounge - popular music venue on Bathurst. St.

Last Dance

EDDY DAVID

Driving home – 4 o'clock in the morning; she's curled up in your jacket, snuggled tight in the seat belt, with her head against the window. A glint of moonlight shows through the window setting a halo effect around her, it was like sitting next to an angel. The road was wet after a midnight summer shower. She lives deep in the east end of the city, while you live in the west. You reminisce about tonight's events.

Laughing it up with your boys, making fun of how your fellow partygoers danced, smiling ear to ear. There was a certain sweetness in the air. She walked in, walked past you, without even saying a word; well at least nothing that was directed to you. Laughing, drinking, eating and dancing with every guy in the place without even giving you a glance.

Who would have known that you had been seeing each other for the past few months? You laughed together, shared your dreams, and cried with each other when you shared your pains. Then one day she up and says she wants to see other people. Your pride discourages you from objecting and you reply "fine!" Hey, you were going to suggest it yourself. She just beat you to it. Two weeks go by without a word to each other. Every time you answer the phone, you answer calling her name, only to be disappointed.

Tonight, you were at the same party and she was ignoring you. Your thoughts and memories bring you close to tears. The DJ tells the ladies to choose their partners for the last dance. You make your farewells and begin towards the door. You then feel a sudden pull against your arm. You try to pull away not realizing who it is, but then stop in your tracks as you hear an angelic voice saying "May I have this dance?"

> *"Whatever I choose to share, it's straight from the heart of a human to the heart of each individual reader or audience."*
>
> **– Kwame Stephens, Poet, Writer, Educator**

sai

HAJILE "LOTUS" KALAIKE

aware of and in harmony
with the True Reality

i feel you
without
help of hands

i taste you
without
use of tongue

i see you
without
need of eyes

realize

i love you
beyond
limit of heart

because
your spirit

your spirit...

your spirit

is softer
than mink fur

your spirit

is sweeter
than pure honey

your spirit

is brighter
than neon colours

our spirits

compliment each other
with a bond stronger than
physical earthly marital

we are

Spiritual
Lovers

Had I Had Locks

MAKI MOTAPANYANE

This is not the poem I intended for you
I wished us beautiful
the kind of beauty born of
the elemental combinations
of browns, cocoa and beige
I wished us like hot chocolate and cocoa-pecan ice cream
in coffee-coloured waffle cones
I had a jones
I had a jones that you sniffed out, picked up
cradled and put to sleep while I
was bottom facing sky head in the bottom of my handbag
looking for that special lipstick
damn!

You liked my hair
because it's got
that kind of ambiguousness that's neither
loose twirl nor tight curl
it screams marginality while remaining
undecidedly mysterious about its
rooted origins

You disliked my hair
Because it's got
that kind of ambiguousness that remains
undecidedly mysterious
it begs the question of loyalty
roots-origin

Maybe you would have more trust in me
if my hair was locked
probably not
Maybe you would proclaim me African Queen
and lay the legacy of our foremothers
at my feet
Maybe you would find Yemoja in my eyes
and Nefertiti in my speech
I have my doubts
you do not recognize me
and I have grown bored
of my own militaristic imperatives to
coax you into seeing me
as you

I feel you feel I am not black enough
You feel I feel you
incomprehensibly ignorant
negligently counterproductive
dangerously regressive
we've come to a standstill
you are suggesting the revolution
requires corn rows
I am suggesting the revolution
requires soldiers

Our Pan-Africanist courtship finds itself
at a crossroads
and we part ways knowing
your cultural nationalism seemingly incomplete
my guerilla tactics extreme to you

My mind tells me my political
physical and spiritual allegiance to liberation
must manifest as a revolutionary change
in thought lifestyle
and you imply the problem
is my hairstyle

You might have been down had I had locks

My Woman and I Say a Prayer Together

STEVEN GREEN

My woman and I say a prayer together
My woman cuts the heart out of the earth for me
Boiling sweet potatoes in a little black pot
Fitting my guts like a glove
Squeezing the bees buzzing inside 'em
I sit at the kitchenette
Sharpening my sword she made from the cloth of her kente dress

My man and I say a prayer together
My man sifts gold out of the dirt for me
Brewing tea in a tiny kettle
He drums on my swollen tummy
Knocking on a door
Settling my nerves like leaves to the ground
I lean on the counter top
Reading his writing in Sanskrit hidden on the front page of the newspaper

The Calabash

NANA YEBOAA

An unbroken calabash is useful for drinking palm wine
The sweet nectar that quenches the thirst of an African man
And soothes his soul from the barrenness of this earth
But a broken calabash is only useful for scraping the burnt pot

Do not disappoint me
Do not make me feel useless
Do not break me into useless bits
Easy to discard like pieces of glass
For the broken calabash even has its use

Make me useful
Make me that special one
Make me the one whom you wash and store in that special place
Make me your precious, of whose bosom's heavenly waters you will savor

The sight of me you should yearn
The touch of me on your lips, should be the honey you swallow
Let me be the one who quenches the heat in your groin
Let me be the one who flatters your heart
Let me be the one whom you wake up to

In a cool shade let me stand
Give me a life full of love
Of which its coolness replenishes your thirst
Give me an unending trust
Give me unsurpassable hope and pleasure
And I will be there whenever you come back

My love is yours to maintain and keep
All I ask is that you make me the vessel that keeps your love
Quarrels should not end our relationship
What bonds us together is more than human flesh

It hurts me when we have a misunderstanding
Sometimes it feels like the air I breathe is withdrawn
You have become an integral part of me
And the heavens surely know that when you leave
You will sap the strength out of my life
Here I leave you to decide
You know my love is with you and my trust you have
I plead you not to destroy

Growing Up in Love

JEDDIAH ISHMEL

I remember as a young boy
I thought love was easy

Love was the ways the world amazed
Love was summer days
In sprinkler sprays
Love was the pure joy of warm sunrays

Love was what I was seeing
Love was what I was hearing
Love was just a feeling

But my mama said

        "Boy that ain't Love
        "Love is trust,
        You ain't even scraped the crust"

        "Though
        It's gonna getcha
        Yes, Love is gonna getcha"

Who me?

        "Yes you, Love is gonna getcha"

I said, Uh-uh Love, I won't letcha

T-Dot Griots

I remember as a young teen
Love was a crush

Love was stars in the eyes
Butterflies in the gut
Sneaking kisses on a cheek
And wishing for luck

'cause
Love was what I was seeing
Love was what I was hearing
Love was just a feeling

But my mama said
                    "Boy that ain't Love
                    "Love is patient
                    You don't fall and peak the same week it went"

                    "But
                    It's gonna getcha
                    Yes, Love is gonna getcha"
Who me?
                    "Yes you, Love is gonna getcha"
I said, Uh-uh Love, I won't letcha

I remember through high school
I thought Love was passion

Love was desire
Love was longing
Love was lust
Love was the closeness built
Through rhythmic thrust

You know
Love was what I was seeing
Love was what I was hearing
Love was just a feeling

But my mama said
　　　　　　"Boy that ain't Love"

I said I know that
But it just sounds like a trap

　　　　　　"Well
　　　　　　It's gonna getcha
　　　　　　Yes, Love is gonna getcha"
Who me?
　　　　　　"Yes you, Love is gonna getcha"
I said, Uh-uh Love, I won't letcha

That's when it cut to the chase
I turned to face, what I thought was Love and girl had a gun
I remembered what Mama said and I broke into a run
I was like hey Love, please Love there must be a misunderstanding
I used to think Love was easy but it had become way too demanding
So I headed for Love's freeway, like the one Aretha told
But it was the 407* and I couldn't pay the toll
So I dilly
Dallied
Dashed into an alley
Bumped into my old girl Sally
From the Valley'
And she said
　　　　　　"I'm all shook up and its all your fault
　　　　　　Your Ma said love was gonna getcha, well you've just been caught."
And I said. . . I can't be your lover
I can't stand game playing
I can't stand crank calling
I can't stand, I can't stand
I can't stand falling

That's when Mama grabbed me by the ear

She said

> "Son you've been through all this
> And you're still going to miss
> 'Love is patient, Love is kind
> Does not envy or boast, that's what Love is
> Its not rude, self seeking
> Easily angered, or list your ails
> It always protects, always trusts
> Always hopes, perseveres and Love never fails'"**

And I said what?

It's gonna get me what
It's gonna get me what
Love come and get me now
It's gonna get me what
Love come and get me now
It's gonna get me what
Oh, come and get me now
Love come and get me. . .

Now here I am a man
Thinking maybe Love is good
Got Mama saying boy I knew you would

Love is real
I can stand up in Love and hold steady
Love ain't got me yet
But I think I'm almost ready

I know now
Love is more than seeing
Love is more than hearing
Love. . . Oh what a feeling

---

* 407 - Electronic Toll Route, highway North of Toronto
** Paraphrased from the Holy Bible,1 Corinthians 13:4-8

Love on Bay Street

YANNICK MARSHALL

I remember
Letting blinds grid my face at the office
Pushed back onto leather chairs
Thumbing portfolios, scattering papers
Chugging mugs full of Maxwell House

See, I've tried to fax my love letters to the paper shredder
Tried to cover my sweat with
Splashes of Aqua Velva, cologne and croissants
Tried to distract myself with packaged potpourri

But it seems you've made a garden of Bay Street;
Have me stepping off the caterpillar, on through revolving glass moths
To jump onto the sliding grasshoppers

You're on my mind like a perfect music mix
As I walk down Front Street
Emptying my briefcase of rosebuds

> "We have the ability to taste dreams and smell laughter so why not do it?"
> – Seth-Adrian Harris, Poetic Filmmaker

> "Tragedy and despair do not have the final say, we do."
> –Melville White, Author
> 'Love Rhapsodies and Blues'

Something to Laugh About

NANA YEBOAA

In gregarious dungeons I was tied
I made love with my hands and legs
In the darkness I discovered the jewel of the night
Like the shine of the moon my precious jewel lit my face
And the sound and rhythms of gumboots
Were applauded with deafening thunder

Away from my family
I made love to the sounds of gushing waters
And to the voices of other men singing to their lovers in faraway places
The thoughts of my sweet Tandoh
I hummed away in the silent night
When the moon brought messages of love

Tidy Ain't Ghetto

CHERYL "NNEKA" HAZELL

She lives in a high-rise in the somewhat seedy-restless-where-gunshots-go-off-in-daylight part of town. Hides out in a 17th floor lair uninterested in urban battles, ethnic cowboys and migratory decay: this is ghetto, but Tidy ain't.

Nasty fatherless boys pee in soapy-chlorine Downy-smelling places, returning the same time next week to check on the stench which a perfumed Tidy smells in the meantime when she plummets 16 stories to do bi-weekly laundry.
And they think I'm ghetto?

While Tidy surfs a cool site sponsored by her brother's credit card there is a scuffle in the hall and she plugs her ears with the *Sounds of Blackness.*
And even though she knows bullets can't reach that high, Tidy taught her tots to run for cover behind enamel remembering to never under-estimate this wild, wild west bordering the ghetto's superhighway. Children's Aid keeps tabs, and kind of thinks she's clueless, but Tidy ain't.

And the banks? Well, the banks love lumping apples and oranges together. According to their list of codes, her location, her classification, her non-gentrification were deemed too ghetto for a gold card, but it ain't and neither is Tidy.

"All skin teeth is not grin", she can hear her great-aunt say. "Patronized, passed over, forced to bow? No, no, sweetie, play the game," she recommends.
So Tidy fakes it, covers up her pride, smiles the smile of cons and gets extra food at Daily Bread, nicer clothes at Sally Anne's, a recommendation from Housing and a tip from the employment counselor.
Idiots.
The system is ghetto but Tidy ain't.

Before You Decided

JASON KINTE

Before you decided, did you know I had plans?
To build nations and lead them; to discover new lands
I speak not of claiming territory inhabited already, instead
I would discover a new state of mind for all that would stop the bloodshed?

Before you decided, did you know what I had on my mind?
Were you aware of the contributions I would make to mankind?
Did you know I would show there is no obstacle in age?
That I would inspire the old to make their appearance on stage?
Did you know I would lead the young, that I would show them the way?
That I would speak to atheists and I would manage to get them to pray?

Before you decided, did you know I would lead?
Thousands to goodness, that I would plant a good seed?
Before you decided, did you know I would protect your mother?
Comfort your dying father and feed your sister and brother?
Before you decided, did you know that you would fall down?
Need help to get up and I would be the only one around?
Before you decided, did you know your daughter would need a brother or sister?
And only I would be there – do you know how much I miss her?

Before you decided to hate me did you know?
Did you consider all of those factors when you ranked me so low?
Did you know before you decided to roll up with your boys and attack?
Did you know before you decided to pull your trigger back?
Did you know before you decided to release it, barrel aimed at my head...
Did you know before you made the calculation that I was better off dead?
Did you know before you decided to lodge a bullet in my brain?
Did you know before you decided to stand there and smile while my blood drained?

Pranksta, before you decided to stab me, did you know?
Gangsta, before you decided to cap me, did you know?
I know you knew how I looked, but trigger-happy police

> *"The message is the only thing that counts. Everything else is vanity."*
>
> **–Unblind Africanus, Griot and Scribe**

Did you know that I was all about peace, before you attacked like a beast?
Crack daddy, did you know that I was going to turn into an angel
Before you gave me that free hit, and sent me to hell?
Crack mommy, before you decided to risk getting me hooked
Did you know that I would become a minister, instead of a crook?
Brother, before you decided to take me to the dope spots
Did you know that I would end up running for the highest office in the land
Instead of just running from the cops?

Parents, *after* you decided to risk having me, but *before* you chose to terminate me
Did you know that I would be the most beautiful baby?
And despite growing up poor, I would turn out amazing?
Before you decided to abort me did you know?

Prayer for the Black Child

KWAME STEPHENS

this is for the black child
born in this country
born into this world
that may help him grow up

this is for the black child
who before the age of twelve
may have a criminal record
for a crime he did not commit

this is for the black child
who will have to struggle
against a white wall
all through his days on earth

this is for the black child
who may grow up into

"Being a griot means having a way with words, bringing people, and places, and things to life. These stories should inspire others, educate them, give them the strength to keep on keepin' on."

– Asha Tomlinson, Journalist

an angry black man
who hates a world which hates him
>if there is something
>you or I can do
>for this black child
>then let us do it
>whatever it is
>may we do our part
>to make this world
>a better place
>a safer place
>for the black child

> *"My message is one of human understanding and forgiveness for the many ways we fall short of perfection and the glory of God."*
> **– Jason Kinte, Founder, Toronto Poets.**

A Still Small Voice in Gen X

DWAYNE SEWELL

Then a small voice within Gen X gasps...

I am dying

Look, as the lost become utterly lost, seeking no liberation
As one without hope
No knowledge of the purpose of his creation
We are truly the generation of vipers
Creators, inspirational singers, writers
Authors and orators of emptiness

We are led and misled by men without chests
Men who betray what they claim in the very same breath
They say God is dead, or he doesn't exist
They laugh at the idea of a heavenly realm
Sadly, I've been to the holy places
Now ruins – and there is no light
No life left in them

So come now fellow vipers
Let us bare our forked tongues
Although our mouths house duplicity
Only smoke comes from our lungs
We will ride on the shoulders of our people
This generation
For we love luscious little lies
We are a people cut off from ourselves
Trying desperately to believe in self
With our backs turned to the skies

We are the champions of all and the believers in nothing
The offenders of no one, the defenders of no one
The brother to every man, but the lovers of our own sins

And the grumbling
Yes the mindless grumbling has lately made me more ill

I am dying,
        I need a drink,
You got a light?
        I need a pill.

We have been made afraid of death but yet it feels so good to kill
Afraid to die but why does it feel so good to kill ourselves slowly
So far removed from holy that we only look forward to self-glory

Now, it's about

I'm gonna get this,
        I'm gonna get that believe me,
I'm gonna be rich
        I'm gonna be phat you'll see me.

We have seen the effects
But have we fully examined the cause?
By this I now take time to reflect
Is it not worthy of pause?

How long shall we go on grasping at straws?
Stumbling in darkness of our own ignorance
Ignoring The Laws
There are universal truths
There are things that are concrete
But in our sweet self -abuse we've managed to cut off our own two feet
Having no foot to stand on, no safe ground to land on
We rely on our common senses
Each to their own
We remain coiled on proverbial fences stranded
Alone
And dying

Love once poured out itself into the darkness of the unlovable and was shown no love
Now we are that rebellious generation, having a form of godliness
But in dying
Denying the power thereof

I am not yet dead
            There is hope

That Negress

MAKI MOTAPANYANE

I am that negress
I bear the trappings
wear the lashings
of a culture hated that feeds
imprisoned souls
this feeding is sustained by options
I am told
buy in or perish

I am that negress
morning-dewed white roses
blooming

from my eye sockets
I am sweating
bleached toilets waxed floors
Pressed clothes stained diapers
from my pores
and you have come to
kindly
inform me I am repelling

You pluck the roses from my eyes
and gift them to your 100% beef burger
bona fide American pie girlfriend
I retreat to engender
re-member
blossom new flowers from
blood stained tears
they are red in hue
you will undoubtedly lay claim
to these too

I am stripped to bare brown flesh
in the town square
that is your mind
from whence my abrasions
are lacerated by all the
confusion curiosity derision
your salt-bathed tongue can muster

I am that negress
your one drop miscegenated nightmare
I carry opalescent dreams
which chameleon at your approach
and you
allow yourself the belief
I have none

they shimmer
a brightness you can not fathom
and fear

After the Show

KAMAU

They walk in my shadow just a few steps behind
And I've walked with them in my shadow so many a time
I've grown accustom to their taunts and their silent tease
They see my skin as my guilt with a violent ease
Predators stalk the night always searching for prey
But I choose not to acknowledge if they have nothing to say

Just another lonely walk home after the shows
That I frequent and speak in sometimes, in my clothes
There's a stench of pain, pleasure and some nicotine
That often permeates the underground poetry scene
I never partake at all but second hand stains my lungs
And when I walk I cough and take shortcuts through the slums

So it's obvious these officers are presuming my guilt
Have descriptions of skin tone and the way that I'm built
That just happen to match every black man in sight
That gives them some excuse whether they're wrong or right
No wonder when I was in school we called police "Beast"
'Cause in my humble city the predators have a feast

Every time that it's night time and often the day
When they see you as criminal in ignorant ways
So in no way at all did it decrease our blues
When we read of racial profiling in the news
'Cause every time I walk in a store I'm followed by eyes
So nobody I know was even vaguely surprised
No black folks at least 'cause some folks didn't know
Unless they walked with us in the streets after the show

> *"I think being black in this country is so full of contradictions. At times we are excluded and invisible, others we're given only negative attentions."*
> – Nadia L. Hohn, Co-ordinator, Iced in Black Film Festival

We Slept in Chinatown

YANNICK MARSHALL

We slept in Chinatown
Under bamboo roofs, Spadina streetcars
And blankets of Shanghai wrappers
We toasted to ginseng under a dragon moon
As bones sprawled out in purified blood
Cleansed with tiger balm
Ain't it beautiful?
Ain't it beautiful?

We are the bums on your street
Ain't it beautiful how our hair glitters like headdresses
As we chase your streetcars?
See, I see y'all still cowboys
Bustling in your corporate saloons, bow legged in late night cafés
Hawking political correctness, into spittoons
Y'all still cowboys
Pistols shooting, blackjack backstabbing
Mission to brrrrrrand us like cows
And have us clinging to change

See tonight we sleep in Chinatown
Tomorrow it will be some other gutter
Where we bend over your apologies scattered like rice
And yes you can watch us from your windows
You could shake your head and tisk tisk like the rain
Y'all tisk tisk
Y'all tisk tisk tisk tisk,
Y'all tisk tisk
like the rain
tisk, tisk
tisk

Can You Give Me a Dollar?

DA ORIGINAL ONE

Can you give me a dollar?
Can you please give me dollar?
  and I will say to you that it is hard being an artist
  and you probably have your stories too
See, some people say that I'm the life of the party
   'cause I tell a joke or two
   but if you take a good look at my face
   and my smile seems out of place
My black ass is sad and blue

Yes it is hard being a Blackman
   and you probably already heard that story too (right?)
As long as I have your attention and this mic
I might as well tell it again
Once upon a time there lived an artist formally known as...
Since
My name has already slipped your mind
I won't waste time
I'm an artist, a poet, a playwright,
   a performer, an actor, a producer etc. etc. etc.
The list could continue, but I don't want to seem conceited
Ultimately, I want to direct
Make a living from what I do and from my peers get some respect

I'm an artist
   and like Warren G says
I want it all
   the house, the money, the car
   a kente colored picket fence
I'm a black man and I got to represent the culture

    No, minimum wage, 'cause if I could pay you less, I would
    Sorry there is a shortage of hours this week
    Business is slow, you know how it is

            funk dat.

Excuse me Massa can I get off the plantation, own my own business
       get benefits with a paid 4 month winter vacation
       so I can be tanning my black butt in the Caribbean
       soaking up the rays of my environment
       with soccer and cricket on the beach
       steel pan music in my ear drum
       and the constant sight of beautiful brown sugar women?
I'm probably asking for too much, huh?
but where is my 40 acres and my 9 yards?
I'm getting older and I just want to know
       can I be loved black and complicated as I am?

I am an artist
Can you give me a dollar?
Can you please give me a dollar?
       'cause a brotha's got to hustle
       and then someone
       told me sex sells ... so I got me some!
Made me a prophet
       where I spoke from the Mount Donald's top
       of my short incoming of cries
       where two diplomas from higher education later
           still asking the questions , do you want a shake with your fries?
What I'm hearing is foul
       a two point dunk on me of trifling and pathetic
       bouncing my balls into court
       with a plea to Your Honour that "truth be told"
       that I can barely pay my rent much less my child support
       but tell me if this ain't wild
       that the repayment of my student loan
       is more important to the government than feeding my child
The rumors are as follows:
       they heard me on the radio
       saw me in the video
       but went over to their friends house to dub off the CD though

I am an artist
Can you give me a dollar?
Can you please give me a dollar?
I'm trying to do what a man is supposed to do
     with the talents that God has blessed me with
     what the hell does my child know about being a starving artist?
I am the artist why does he have to starve?

Now you're looking at me talking about
     brotherman seems like you trying to crossover
     and I say hell yeah
     'cause on that side of the street I can go to the bank
     gain more interest, get a toaster, a calendar
     and feel no way when I get their token thanks
I've been on this side of the street begging for a dollar
It's only when you need my help do you know me or call me brother

I am an artist
Can you give me a dollar?
Can you please give me a dollar?
     not as a hand out but what is due to me
That dollar is to feed my family

In the Darkest Hour
hERONJONSE

In the darkest hour
Electric currents stream through high voltage cities
Blue screens flicker as late night fiends plug into vision machines
Many try to sleep, midnight lovers creep
Insomniacs pop pills to kill their wake state
Pleasure seekers pop pills to enhance their dream state
Philosophers meditate between puffs and float on clouds of insight

Watching club goers prescribe medicinal melodies
Breaking away from the stresses of the day
Corporations crack the whip for the midnight shift
Moneymakers fight to keep their eyes open while
Money-takers knife through purses and wallets and cut out of sight
Into the bowels of the night
Conspirators conspire under cigarette lights
Vagabonds search for the warmth of a fire
Search for desire but find a bittersweet, long kiss goodnight on the concrete
Long kisses from business ladies who hate credit
Trying to avoid charges but accepting cash
To perform the consumer's twisted sexual fantasies
Fathers and sons hunt for little sexies
They drink the hypnotic and envision women
Slithering across stages and shedding their skins

In the darkest hour when the venom starts to soak in
That's when I begin
To spiral into mental trances
Electric currents stream through nerve centres
Impulses flicker the screens of my vision machine
I can't sleep, urges creep through my wake state
Medicinal memories of past pleasures pop like pills and enhance my dream state
For insight I meditate on puffy clouds, allow the stresses of the day to float away
Incorporated cravings work the graveyard shift
I fight to keep my eye open as they knife in and out of sight into the bowels of my mind
These vagrant vagabonds conspire to light fires of desire
Sparking long kisses which are more bitter than sweet
The motions made to avoid these charges are the same that fuel their twisted fantasies
Immune to their hypnotic drink
I envision, the stages which shed light
In the darkest hours I find
That the activities of the outside world
Are constantly occurring within my mind

My Voice

MAKI MOTAPANYANE

My voice is
the mystic instrument upon which
I sound my divinity

> *"Share your words, you never know who you will inspire."*
> **– Kathleen James, Poet**

My voice measures the degree to which
I enter your political calculations
and universal interpretations
to which I bite into your intellectual
and spiritual constellations

My voice is this poet's tree

My voice sounds the urgency
of all I do and don't want you to see

My voice is the tree whose fruit
buds you free
My fruit is the food whose roots lie
in the soil of black royalty
My food is the voice with which
I urge you to see

My voice is this revolution's
form of currency
My currency is the urgency with which
I buy my mind out of white normalcy

My voice is the instrument with which
I sound black bodies in a state of emergency
My emergency is that we are a commodity
My emergency is that commodities
have no country
My country is the dollar brand
that is killing me softly
My killing is the brand I buy
with my dollar love conformity

My voice is the tear that sounds
its search for community

My voice is the community
that sounds its search for unity

My voice is the poetry
that sounds my family tree
My family tree is the voice
that tongues our history

My voice is the spear
that tongues me free

"Griots are sharp witted and breathe the spirit of their community. They are the voice of their respective cultures."
– heronJonse, Poet, Journalist

All Worked Out

KAREN RICHARDSON

I've got it all worked out.
Don't you want to be like me?
I know who I am, where I am and where I'm going.
I know everyone worth knowing and they're only going to make me better
At being a know it all, see it all, and be it trendsetter
I don't plan to change the world, but I wouldn't be surprised if I did
I see the awe in the eyes of them star struck kids when they see me
If I wasn't who I am
I'd wanna be me
I've got it all worked out, you must be blind if you don't see me

Step 1: I'm moving out to New York City I'm a get myself a stylist to make my hair pretty. Like those girls in the shows. Those girls with high class designer clothes. Those girls who wave an ounce of some drink I can't pronounce, in them hip-hop videos. Don't get me wrong, I rep my city. I love T.O., but it's a pity. They just can't do hair the way them States cats do. It's true. When, they perm it, weave it, gel it, leave it. Ah come on, you see it too! And the dudes down there, hey! It's the American way. The build them Ford tough with all them little cute things they say.

I've got it all worked out.
Don't you want to be like me?
I know who I am, where I am and where I'm going.
I know everyone worth knowing and they're only going to make me better
At being a know it all, see it all, and be it trendsetter
I don't plan to change the world, but I wouldn't be surprised if I did
I see the awe in the eyes of them star struck kids when they see me
If I wasn't who I am
I'd wanna be me
I've got it all worked out, you must be blind if you don't see me

Step 2: It won't take long for me to make my debut. I'll get a fat contract then I'll fly down my crew. It's not new. 'You know how us Canadians do'. I'll get through. They already know we got it going on –Glenn Lewis, Nelly Furtado, Celine Dion...but me, I'm making my big break in R&B. I'll get really comfy on the couch with AJ and Free, in the number one spot on the BET top ten. You done know I'm gonna be there often, just as soon as Little X discovers me. But how could he not? I have everything those other girls got. Trust me, X will holler. And I'll compensate for what I'm missing, once I start to get my hands on that American dollar.

I've got it all worked out.
Don't you want to be like me?
I know who I am, where I am and where I'm going.
I know everyone worth knowing and they're only going to make me better
At being a know it all, see it all, and be it trendsetter
I don't plan to change the world, but I wouldn't be surprised if I did
I see the awe in the eyes of them star struck kids when they see me
If I wasn't who I am
I'd wanna be me
I've got it all worked out, you must be blind if you don't see me

Step 3: I'll bring new meaning to that old word "paid". Special Ed ain't the only one who's got it made. When I sell four million records, I'll be more popular than Princess Diana. But I won't let it get to my head – I'll bless my home town with my float at Caribana. Just like Shaq. I'll model, I'll rap, no doubt I'll act. You can't be a megastar with just one hit track, unless you're Miss Keys. Oh please, the album was okay, but four Grammies?

I digress, folks have made it big with much less, that's why I know this music thing is no contest.

I've got it all worked out.
Don't you want to be like me?
I know who I am, where I am and where I'm going.
I know everyone worth knowing and they're only going to make me better
At being a know it all, see it all, and be it trendsetter
I don't plan to change the world, but I wouldn't be surprised if I did
I see the awe in the eyes of them star struck kids when they see me
If I wasn't who I am
I'd wanna be me
I've got it all worked out, you must be blind if you don't see me

To Slam or Not to Slam

DWAYNE MORGAN

Whether it be classic hip hop battles, dance hall clashes or calypso extempos, there is nothing more thrilling for an audience than to watch their favourite artists using their creativity to win over the crowd and show off their creative brilliance. So too in the world of spoken word a practice exists to encourage competition.

At poetry slams, the spoken word artist is given three minutes to impress judges, selected from the audience, with their delivery and on-stage presence. The poetry slam began as a way to remove the barrier between the audience and the artist, thus incorporating onlookers into the art. While some debate the origin of the slam, it is widely credited to Marc Kelly Smith, host at the Green Mill in Chicago, Illinois.

I've seen poetry slams conducted in several ways in my travels as a spoken word artist. They bring the audience into the event, having them offer cheers, applause or scores in support of their favourite artist or the competitor who impresses them the most.

Since their inception, poetry slams have spread throughout the world, creating a vibrant network of stages, where the most creative wordsmiths can travel and test their skills against other artists. Such slams take place throughout Europe, with notable ones occurring in England and Germany. Large competitions include the All German Speaking Countries Slam and the All Europe Slam. On this side of the pond one will encounter the Vancouver slams and of course, The Nationals.

The 'Nationals' occur annually in the United States at a time of year when the lyrics are fierce and the performances are filled with passion and energy. Teams from across the United States and

Canada compete for lyrical supremacy. Artists practice, train and vie for the chance to participate in the National slam. The exercise helps to ensure the artists constantly improve the quality of their work, so they peak and have their best work and best possible performance ready for slam time.

To date, Vancouver, Winnipeg and Ottawa are the only Canadian cities that participate in the Nationals. Shane Kocyzan, a member of the Vancouver slam team, is the only non-American to ever win the National Poetry Slam Individual Championship. When viewing the Canadian landscape, Toronto has always been heralded for its art and artistic community, but this stops when it comes to the spoken word.

Where does Toronto fit into all of this? Toronto barely really factors into the overall North American spoken word marketplace as there is no slam venue that exists and few artists on the small slam circuit. As a result, many of the artistic offerings from this city's spoken word artists, lack the creativity and energy of their American and global counterparts.

Not only does the slam excite and include the audience, but it also creates a forum through which the artist can compare their work to that of their peers, possibly developing friendly rivalries and forcing one another to dig deeper into their minds, their souls and their creative arsenal to constantly create art that is beyond even their wildest expectations of themselves.

For a city of its size, it is unfortunate that Toronto lacks a slam scene, and even more unfortunate that many of the offerings at local open mics leave a lot to be desired when one is searching for something beyond the ordinary. The question remains: to slam or not to slam? The future of Toronto's spoken word scene hangs in the balance, awaiting our response.

The King of the Slam

R. OSAZE DOLABAILLE

I'm the King of the Slam
that's who I am
the winner, the champion, the number one poet
feeling really inadequate, but I don't even know it
yet I have to be better than
to look down upon
somebody else
or else I feel exposed
for the people would see me
instead of who I want to be
and that cannot be allowed

so I'll go on proclaiming
and keep right on naming myself
the King of the Slam

Always so competitive
I have to be the best
better than all the rest
at what exactly?
It doesn't matter
poetry is alright, I guess
black history sells well
sex is useful too
I've been beaten down for so long
don't know what else to do
when the people see me
do they ever wonder
about what kind of pain is laying just under
this mask that I wear?
but we won't go there right now
'cause at the end of the day
all I have left to say
is I am
the King of the Slam

Another poet is over there throwing down
the people are really feeling him
damn!
I can't stand the success of that brother
I must think I am superior to every other
or else I feel worthless
because I am jealous
it's exhilarating to get praise and applause
my frail ego needs boosting
and that is because
of an empty heart that refuses to share
I want it all for me
so I can continue to be
known as
the King of the Slam

R. Osaze Dolabaille, La Parole, 2003

I know!
I'll play the consciousness game
walk around in the colours, choose an African name
that should get all the girlies drooling
but the desired effect always wears off
I don't want to face the real ugly truth
that I'm laughed at by elders
and ignored by the youth
the people can tell I'm a fraud and it angers me
but I can't change now
I really need this label
so that I am able
to say
I'm the King of the Slam

I'm the King of the Slam
I'm the King
Me, not we
cramming through the spoken word
jamming on the groupies
slamming the people every chance that I get
pretending I'm righteously angry
and yet
the sisters see through it all
I hate them for that
I ought to slam them too
in fact
I'll even slam all of you
if you ever get in my way!!
Because...
I'm the King of the Slam

Sunset

R. OSAZE DOLABAILLE

They used to say the sun never set on their empire
Do you remember?

They proclaimed it day and night
backed up with terrifying weaponry
until the rest of us believed it would always be that way
natural notions of cyclical time
suddenly punctured through
by the phallic thrust of western inevitability

We learned to rely on their concept of God
for comfort and direction
completely unaware
that we were actually worshipping the enemy

With crucifix in the left hand
and firearm in the right
they played out their drama of deceit time and again
vast regions were overrun
entire peoples subjugated, kidnapped, enslaved

Mother Earth herself dishonoured
the sacred womb carved up
torn apart
while the fangs of the colonizer went deep
to seek out the lifeblood within

When this became bothersome and unproductive
they trained up their brainwashed minions
living, breathing corpses
to man the decaying infrastructures
so that wealth would continue to flow to the European
and the sun would continue to shine

But the sun does not stay in the sky for anybody

As proof of their triumph
they would point with pride
to colour-coded maps
indicating which area of the globe had become infected
by which group of "explorers", so called
and those from one island nation in the North Atlantic
exceeding all others in self-congratulation
wrote the textbook on how to perpetuate the infestation
beating their peculiar language
into succeeding generations of victims
creating within us a distorted sense of identity
with the oppressor
instead of against, which would lead to our freedom

Disconnected from the wisdom of ages
our void was filled with their poison
we learned to sing their songs
to read their books
and think their thoughts
until we were actually able to see ourselves as they do
as backwards
lazy
good-for-nothing people
who had been out in the sun too long

But now who is suffering from sunburn?
What do we see all around us today?

Globalized economy
orgies of pollution and destruction
in pursuit of material gain
whose foundation cannot withstand a little pressure
if the price of fuel begins to rise?

Internet technocracy
seeking to plug the whole world into the machine
as long as there are no computer viruses
and what would we all ever do
if the power goes out for good?

Bioengineered food and medicine
designed to improve upon
that which has already been provided by the Creator
but is itself creating
new and insidious ways for people to suffer and die

And let us not forget the sacred twin pillars
of "Freedom" and "Democracy"
which they are so quick to jump up and say
the rest of us should be upholding
while their own hypocritical practices
reveal the W-Bush-league nature
of white supremacy

You see
They used to say that the sun would never set on their empire
but even now
the shadows are lengthening...

> *"Throw ah eye on the steelpan."*
> **– Jesse P. Andrews, The Pan Poet**

From "Steal" Drum to Steel-drum

JESSE P. ANDREWS

De African drum is de African mouth
When de drum talking a spirit jump out
It go in your mind then it go down your spine
And de African spirit make you wriggle and wine

So you wriggle and wine as de drums converse
But de colonial masters dem did fear the worse
Dem say how the drums talking war
So they ban the drums from shore to shore

But de African spirit never leave de land
It jump in a goat then it went in a man
Then it fly in a fowl and end in a pan
Now de steelpan drum is the Trini mouth

And when de pans playing the spirit dance out
It go in your mind then it go down your spine
And de steelpan spirit make you wriggle and wine
You wriggle and wine as de high note ring
And ah Griot say "pan is a spiritual ting."

"*Great influence on my writing is my heritage.*"
– *Kwame Stephens, Poet, Writer, Educator*

He Used To Hear Tales

JANE MUSOKE-NTEYAFAS

He used to hear tales
About a tiny tropical island
That sat in the realms of the Caribbean
Decorated with coconut and palms trees
That lined its shorelines like seashells
The little Canadian boy would sit by his grandmother
And hear her colourful stories
About the fertile spits of terra cotta land
Bordered by turquoise waters

He used to hear tales
About the plunging purple precipices
Of the Morne de Salle peak
Tallest of the jade mountain ranges
Of a terrain once known as Saint-Domingue
The little Canadian boy would sit by his grandmother
And hear her colourful stories
About the hibiscus and orchid flowers
And the bottle deep emerald valleys

He used to hear tales
About the plush polished beaches
The indigo-black lagoons
The myriad of inlets and beautiful bays
And the night lights of Port au Prince

The little Canadian boy would sit by his grandmother
And hear her colourful stories
Of cloud kissing forests and jungles
With leaves that covered the water's edge

He used to hear tales
Of his caramel and jet black ancestors
Of the precious jewel where she was birthed
Her eyes glittering with fading memories
He heard about the language of Creole
The little Canadian boy would sit by his grandmother
And hear her colourful stories
About the bending rivers and creeks
The swamps lazily sliced by waterways

He used to hear tales
Of his honey sweet origins
Tales of Haïti

> *"[The inspiration for] my pieces related to African-Canadian history, come from the lack of information taught in schools."*
> **Kathleen James, poet**

The Missing Pages in Canadian History
KATHLEEN "STRONG" JAMES

"Heritage Moment" refers to the 60-second mini-movies broadcast on Canadian television where important stories from Canada's past are dramatized. Produced by the Historica Foundation, the first one "Underground Railroad" debuted a decade ago. Currently, there are more than sixty unique minutes.

Somewhere between a "Heritage Moment" and black fly
It is here Canadian history lies
Somewhere between a "Heritage Moment" and black fly
It is here Canadian history lies

Little or no mention of Mathew Da Costa, the translator, explorer and navigator
What about Olivier Le Jeune, the first known person to be enslaved here?
And just a page in a textbook for Marie-Joseph Angélique
Because knowledge of black history is confined to a few weeks – in February
Even worse, there is so much emphasis on events in the U.S.
That this leads us to be ignorant of the Canadian context

And hey, it shouldn't be that way
Especially since black history in Canada is about more than just enslavement and discrimination
It's about the building of this nation, migration and the accomplishments
Of Henry Bibb the founder of "The Voice of the Fugitive"
Mary Ann Shadd, North America's first black female publisher
Elijah McCoy the inventor and William Hall who won the Victoria Cross
John Ware, the cattle rancher and William Hubbard
How did all this history get lost?

It did when somewhere between a "Heritage Moment" and black fly
Canadian society decided to perpetuate the lie of
A history that is glorified and satirized but never criticized
Or the image of Canada the benevolent and Canada the great
Is it too late? Can the damage that's been done be reversed? Or is this a curse?

This is why we know little or nothing about
The Black Loyalists, the Maroons and the African Rifles in BC
The black soldiers that fought in both world wars for you and me
The coal mine workers, Stanley Grizzle and the black car porters
Don Moore and the NCA fighting for changes in the immigration laws
Isaac Phills, Viola Desmond, domestic workers
Rosie Douglas, Rodney John and racism at Sir George Williams
Minnijean Brown Trickey, Little Burgundy
Africville, Priceville, Negro Creek and Hugh Burnett
There is so much Canadian history
I hope I will never forget
The struggles of my people

There are other groups whose accomplishments remain unknown
Could you imagine what Canadian history would be like if all of the missing stories were told?
I often wonder how the truth would unfold
Until Canadian society can come to terms with its past
The absented presence of many in Canadian history will continue to last

Now I must teach and ensure that my knowledge will reach as many as will hear
It still seems like a long time before all unheard voices will appear
In textbooks, in TV shows and in movies
And do you know why? It's because Canadian history is being depicted as
being somewhere between a "Heritage Moment" and black fly

O Canada

KATHLEEN "STRONG" JAMES

The national anthem of Canada also bears the title "O Canada". Composed by Quebecois music teacher Calixa Lavalée. He was commissioned to set a French language poem by Judge Adolphe-Basile Routhier to music. The song was first played for the Congrès National de Canadiens-Français on June 24, 1880. Many English versions were written before Robert Stanley Weir penned the 1908 lyrics, which are used currently with minor changes. A motion was passed in parliament on January 31, 1966 by Prime Minister, Lester B. Pearson, that "That the government be authorized to take such steps as may be necessary to provide that 'O Canada' shall be the National Anthem of Canada while 'God Save the Queen' shall be the Royal Anthem of Canada."

More than cold weather, igloos, moose, Mounties and pine trees
There are people here of all races
Who come from different places
However, racism exists here
It's subtle, but racism is present here
In spite of this country's diversity
There are problems in each city

Whether you are stopped for no reason on the street by police
Who believe you fit the description of the criminal they are looking for
Choosing to ignore that you are
three inches taller and a little bit smaller than the guy they should still be searching for
But hey, you're black so it doesn't matter
Because the policy is
Arrest now and ask questions after
In the land of friendly people, Canada Dry and Molson beer

Here, one's status or level of education
Does not exempt you as a black person from discrimination
At some point you become aware of the systemic racism
In the workplace or even in the educational system
Such as textbooks that omit the presence of the black race
When our people live here and have existed here for many years
Although we may be in some areas small in number, we exist here
We have helped to build this society
And at the political level we have helped to form new policies

But the image of this country is exclusive
And blacks are not included
In the definition of being Canadian which includes
Caucasian, English and French speaking, peace keepers

On the other hand
In some respects Canada is the Promised Land
Full of opportunities
Compared to many countries
But sometimes when I think of this land which is supposed to be "glorious and free"
And accepting of everybody
I am reminded of the actions of groups and individuals
Contradictory to the Charter of Human Rights and Freedoms
"Everyone is equal before the law"
Sure

Oh Canada!
The acts and bills written in Ottawa on Parliament Hill are failing to protect us!
So we must work together
Rally together
Inform others who do not know
About the injustices done to our people
Then we will begin to move beyond the image of Canada containing
Ice sculptures, a huge land mass with
Caucasian, peace-keeping, friendly people, moose, igloos, Canada Dry, Molson beer
Mounties and pine trees

KKKanada

MALIK I.M.

In this land of the strong and free
Through patriot's eyes that look in fear
Because the dirty secret that is buried
Has resurrected itself to make something clear
That the ways of our southern neighbours
Have been our ways for centuries
Yet no one has bothered to look up here

The quasi-liberal great white north
That enslaved African-Americans thought was heaven
Removed from a hell south of the 49th

To catch a glimpse of freedom and his brethren
Only to lose themselves in the matrix of this cultural labyrinth
The façade of equality, liberty, and opportunity
Reared its ugly head with impunity
Because this true north, strong and free
An image assembled to distort the truth
Only two-thirds of the world can uproot
History's festering wounds exposed to the air
The defamation of Chinese and Indian railway builders
The "enemy alien" Japanese of the war years
Villified out of distrust, envy, and fears
The racially segregated communities in Nova Scotia and Ontario
The Maple Leaf and Jim Crow
Actions identical to our star-spangled peers

Outside of Vancouver, Toronto, and Montreal
Where is this messiah called multiculturalism?
Sent to smite racist potential
Making the meek stand tall
To stand on top of this vertical prism
Making self-determination the threat to all
Who disguise their ignorance as wisdom

Our home and native land?
Remember the First Nations we decimated
Their bodies, cultures, and histories cremated
Placed on reserves where they remain devastated
Looming over their still bodies
The northern exposure that slaughtered their fates
The apartheid of annihilation awaits
Life, liberty, and security of person are forsaken
The shadowy figure of Inequality
With a toothless smile
And sightless stare
Governed by hatred
For the visible scare
To keep the public in perpetual fright
KKKanada forgets that being colour-blind
Means she can only see black and white

Melanin

UNBLIND AFRICANUS

Imagine absolute darkness
Through which your eyes could only see
Obscurity
The full light spectrum
Evaporated into a section
As the pineal gland pushes manifestations
And absorbs all light
Hence we dark
Shining obscurity
Enlightened divinity
From progenitor to progeny
Kemetically embedded
Genetically perpetuated philosophy
So my knots contracted
And no lye can substitute for my heritage connected
Heat conducted
Sun rays absorbed
So we ain't hyphenated
But hyper-melanated
Multi-faceted metabolisms
Djembes determine the hearts rhythm
All deficiencies are mel-anomalies
The sounds of thoughts
Dissipate earthly tonalities
Enriching monotonous trivialities
Caught in the prism of our divining melanin
Solutions lie in sinking beyond the skin
Digging
Into multiple levels of interior lining
Reflected in the mind's chemical combining
So we vegetarian carnivores
Unnatural reservoirs
For those lacking divining melanin
In the frailness of un-thick skin
Little do they know that our thickness of completion
Lies without and within
Carbon bonded to our melanin
Carbon bonded to our melanin

She Wore

JANE MUSOKE-NTEYAFAS

She wore
The strings of her hair
In tight dyed braids
And slick weaves
Of worm woven silken texture
Imported from the scissor-cut heads
Of Chinese factory women

She wore
The irises of her eyes
In tinted shades
Of Indigo blue like evening skies
And emerald green lenses
Hiding the caramel essence
Of her own eyes

She wore
The coating of her skin
In bleached mulberry hues
Kissed by lightening creams
That had transformed her
Mahogany-copper-red-boned complexion
Into sandy remnants of her former self

She wore
Her African soulfulness
Behind a façade of whiteness
Disowning the last vestiges of her heritage
With the impact of her actions
She was what she was not
And she called it being real

> **"[My work is] intended for the whole world, but as far as inspirations [and] messages, my audience is anyone of African decent, especially women."**
> **– Jane Musoke-Nteyafas, Poet and Visual Artist**

Jane Musoke-Nteyafas, La Parole, 2003

126

Little Wimmin

KAREN RICHARDSON

Eleven year old little black queen
Training brassiere and low-rider jeans
Insider info
At the outsider age
Her second floor bedroom feels like a cage
Last Christmas instead of toys she requested clothes
On New Year's Eve she told her mother how to do her cornrows
First child
A good kid
She's the responsible one
By Valentine's she went to the salon to get it done

"It's not fun looking like this I get so angry I could blow up
Why can't she accept that I'm gonna have to grow up
Won't let me airbrush my nails, get a perm
Or wear makeup
Mommy better watch it 'cause one day I might just take up and go
I've had enough of the prisoner's life
If I don't look sexy, no one will want me for a wife
Looking like a child
I look like a child"

She looks like a child
And for a while I forgot that she is
Reminding me to 'keep it on the low' while she tells me her biz
Motherhood has got to be a whole different world
Raising a black female who doesn't want to be a girl

And to think...
Little girls just wanna be wimmin
Don't blink
You might miss all the little fish swimming
Upstream in a school of hard knocks
On the blocks
Playing big people games
Talking big people talks

After school she throws down the books and picks up the phone line
Switches the TV to channel forty nine
Every lyric, every song, every dance she knows
Learning less from her school teacher
Than the models in the shows
And who knows?
I think she thinks we think
That's all there is to living
Posing, drinking, shaking, pimping
Making sure the men are giving
Us girls lots of attention
As we're showing off our bodies
Too young to understand that it's an overrated party

She's a smarty pants in a diva stance
With less knowledge than she has lip
No respect for Mother's guidance

> *"I think she's on an ego trip*
> *forcing me to slow down*
> *she's on some 'act your age' tip*
> *Mommy better chill 'cause I have things to see*
> *And acting like a child isn't really helping me*
> *She makes me act like a child*
> *I act like a child"*

She acts like a child
And for a while I forgot that she is
Reading me the questions to the Cosmo quiz
Give mothers some credit
You said it's easy
Bite your tongue
Have you ever raised a girl who doesn't want to be young?

And to think...
Little girls just wanna be wimmin
Don't blink
You might miss all the little fish swimming
Upstream in a school of hard knocks

On the blocks
Playing big people games
Talking big people talks

Mother's Day rolled by and they rang it in with shouting
Mother put her foot down and daughter ran off pouting
'Cause she couldn't catch a flick

"I'm so sick of her
She doesn't make sense,
he's tall, he's seventeen and he's got his license
If she thinks she can shelter me
It's already much too late
I know what to do when you go on a date
What's her problem?
Mommy always has her panties in a bunch
Wait till my birthday she can't stop me then
'Cause after twelve is lunch.
She makes me live like a child
I live like a child"

She lives like a child
And for a while I forgot that she is
Watching her make Jell-O
Just to practice how to kiss
Motherhood these days must be a whole heap of stress
Fighting for the childhood of your own little miss

Not getting any younger
You can see the hunger in her eyes
Because she wants to be a woman
And she can't despite her tries
Let the girls be girls
Free from hyper-sexualized interference
At age eleven she's too young to be hung up on her appearance
Or at 12 or 13, 14, 15, 16 even more
Girls, please learn to love yourselves
Don't rush what is in store

There's a natural ebb and flow to life
And when tides change, there will be others
Save yourself the heartache
Heed the wisdom of your mothers

And to think...
Little girls just wanna be wimmin
Don't blink
You might miss all the little fish swimming
Upstream in a school of hard knocks
On the blocks
Playing big people games
Talking big people talks

i wish?
KEVIN REIGH

now, it's not just the cow
but mankind jumping over the moon

soon silver spoons will scoop minerals from stars
one small step
a giant leap from here to mars – and beyond
I guess it's only on planet earth
where grass is greener on the other side
maybe its just greener from rocket fuels and pesticides
I remember when god had a green thumb
but now the green thumb is inside of a machine
                    I used to wish upon a star, now I wish with my satellite dish

the shortest distance between two points
used to be a straight line
now it's a virtual destination at the click of a finger
went from mail to document delivery to electronic mail to email
soon to be just "e"
designer narcotic

say no to drugs
but yes to technology
human biology, like pop psychology or pop music
available for download on the internet

politicians, scientists, laymen don't believe in interracial dating
yet in your salad bowl they have the genes of salmon and tomatoes mating
debating the wave of the future
connectivity between human beings
3-way calling
2-way paging
1-way they'll all be obsolete it seems
but never fear
with the right cable provider
you can have technicolour and surround sound in your dreams
                                        I used to wish upon a star, now I wish with my satellite dish
hundreds of us
thousands of us
millions of us
are hooked on technology like phonics from an embryonic stage

tech-knowledg-y
they've separated the knowledge
but left only the tech
hi-tech, low tech
I even detect it on the breath of infants
no more pablum
no baby formula
not even a breast to feed
indeed
baby mommas give their children cell phones
before they give them books to read
computer illiterate but well read
the last of a dying breed
I've heard it said you reap what you sow
but what could we possibly reap
if a machine plants the seed?

I used to wish upon a star, now I wish with my satellite dish
                                        I used to wish upon a star, now I wish, I wish...

Semen-Dropper

JASON HUMPHREYS KINTE

My name is Semen-Dropper, I drop semen for a living
Y'all may think I'm a villain but I think that I'm giving
And philanthropic – I only drop the highest quality semen
I've mastered a bodily function essential for all of mankind's existence
And y'all make me out as some demon
And I don't understand it

Semen-dropping is an honest occupation
Oh! Hold up!
I think I see a possible site for my semen's incubation
What's up honey? You look sweet
You look like you got a nice pool in which my semen could grow large
Would you like some semen dropped?
I won't even charge...

Free semen-dropping services, call 1-800-Semen-Supreme
And here's my pager number, just in case my semen's busy
Making another honey scream
I'm not just a local Semen-drop–
(Oops, I think I just dropped some there)
I'm not just a local Semen-dropper
I've dropped semen everywhere
From Malvern to Mississauga, Venus to Deep Space Nine
My expertise is rare

Plus my semen's thoroughbred, it's won numerous races
It's even in the Guinness book for the semen that swam the most places
Oh, you don't believe? Do you have a jar?
I'll drop my semen in it and prove that it can swim far!

I remember some time ago a customer tried to stop my semen's flow
The trick pulled out a condom, I said 'Oh no, no, no'
That's like hand-cuffing an artist or not accepting honey from a bee
I'm the famous Semen-dropper, condoms weren't made for me...

Besides – I help people
If you know some guy that's thirty-five
That can't get his wife pregnant because his semen won't survive
Just send him to me, that's my specialty
And if I can't get his semen to live
The least I'll do is give his wife some from me!

I've got endless bounds of semen
Enough to spread all around
Don't tell anybody but there's actually a whole town
Of little boys and girls with my features – they're adorable creatures
Not that I still go to the town...
But their mothers send me pictures
'This is your daughter, now seven; you owe her an eleven thousand dollar cheque'
Man, they're always stressing me...
But I'm the famous Semen-Dropper
Now tell me, what did they expect?

Greenbeans

ERNEST CARTER

Snap like green beans and the clasp on jewels given by the overseer
Stuck like green string in my teeth
Tooth pick'n, chicken grinnin' niggas stuck
Green, not quite ripe
Not yet ready
Naive to the truth led astray 'cause the lead in pencils replaced the crack of the whip

The lash hurts and put perimeters on rebels rousing
The lash can, has and will continue to silence the whine of the squeaky wheels
Understand crack has nothing to do with green beans
Crack has no feet yet it runs over and through tomorrows cure
Itz a nuff dem crack a mon cyan fall true

calously...

blindly...

Still the overseer/officer has fashioned a fetter with a dead bolt form-fitted for your neck
And no one can save you
Steppin' and a fetchin'
Mocked in black face
Making n-i-g-g-e-r an institution
Breaking my spirit curding my stomach
Making me feel uncomfortable

The evil men do
Some sling and stranger fruit swings
Bartering souls stringing out the naive
All for the promise of being hung from a lower tree
With a phat gold link loose
Stuck, pencil whipped
Necks snap like a green bean

"My work is inspired by many things that surround me in Toronto."
– Kwame Stephens, Poet, Writer, Educator

What's Gwaanin'?

DWAYNE SEWELL

I seen a girl get fling down
Two, three times, on Yonge Street
And all the man-dem on the block in front the spot
just kiss dem teet'

Who?
          A nah my business dat
                    Yu no see how de yout' a try walk her out and she still full up a chat!?
Brute!
          Chuck dat!
                    It should have been me

Were some of the words thick in the mix
Up in the soup of the scene
And in between the how you means
Was

What would you do instead?

That was for me and I could tell
It was followed with dread

So there I stood with no plan
Just small hands in each hand
Holding my youts
The young recruits
Already trying to spit truth and

I don't know what's gwaanin'
Was all that I could say

It was a Caribana morning
And I was trying to be brave for my young braves
But I find myself on centre stage
Someone flipped the page
And now I'm fielding questions on rage
From downright amazed
I moved to reeling
Puzzled and dazed
My shadowy gaze
Caught that girl, I hope she's okay

Okay, okay do the right thing
Excite what's right in the minds of these junior kings
Because hooligans grow up to be self-proclaimed kingpins
While some think this is just the drama that Yonge brings
Isn't this something?
This happens yearly on-ya
It's a Yonge Street ting

Well I guess I'm choking now
I can't seem to find words that sound profound and broken down
Like using just a verb and a pronoun
Done dat
'I should have saids are filling my head
Now I'm ready
Yell from on top the spot's awning
                              This is twisted yo
And I still don't know
                    What's gwaanin'?

word?

MOTION

What's the word on the street?
I hear Shaloya got beat
Her moms run her thru the hallway
Call her bitch and a freak
Seem that step-dad's been feeling the heat
Force his hand up under her panties
Made her cry in her sleep
Police screech up to the building round three
But not one ear trying to hear what these eyes won't see
Mom in the cruiser with blood on her hands, wrist in arrest
Shaloya lying in the hallway with a knife in her chest

scene
MOTION

Bright
    airy
and
    nice
the yellow
   walls
hold
  caged men
and freed
   women
who cling
  as the
bell
    rings.

A Chat 'Bout Gun
EVON SMITH

Di bwoy dem a chat 'bout
Dem wan' pick up gun
A true dem no know seh
Di world soon done
Dem fi seek God before dem no have no whey fi tu'n
An dem a chat 'bout which gyal dem a go run:
Patsy, Suzette, Paula, Maxine or Jane?
An' when dem have pickney
dem a go call out fi' yu name
An' when whole heap a pickney
a ring out fi' yu ears hole
A dem time deh
Yu wan' give God control

But nuttin' no wrong wit' dat
Everyt'ing cool
As long as yu no mek no nex' gyal mek you tu'n fool
So when Marla bawl out
Junior!
No pay her no mind
An' if all she a do a beg yu fi' money, don't be kind
Just tell her fi' move and ga'long an fi seek God 'cause
He will mek her strong
An' no badda chat seh yu Christian and yu
Gone a dance a claim seh yu bad man

Hypocrites!
No badda call out God name an'
Go run di rude bwoy game
'Bout yu a pick up gun
Yu t'ink seh yu live life fi' fun?

War. War. War.
SANKOFA JUBA

How come humans neva learn from war?
So many wars

We have World War One
Then we have World War Two
Now we wan' World War Three

War. War. War.
Too much war, Star

World have fought civil wars
That was uncivil
Causing much suffering to civilization

War afar
Causing deep internal scars, Star

Earth has too much wars
Mi wan' move go a Mars

Now dem gone a space
Fi start star wars
While earth have star-vation

When Russia and America use to fight
Dem call it 'Cold War'
Wars in Africa
Dem call it 'Hot War'

War. War. War.
Too much war
Bloody war, jus shed nuff blood
War on crime, no solve crime
War on drugs, neva stop drugs use
But di war goes on

America's constitution gives dem the right to bear arms
But dem a armshouse fi truth
Selling their arms through CIA and FBI to fight poli-trick-al war in Jamaica

Gang war
Too much warriors
Not enough lovers

War. War. War.
Crusade war
Religious war
Holy war
Unholy war, Star
Follow the North-star

Women and children
Suffers the most from war, Star
Suffering from star-vation
Food aid intervention

A no prevention from malnutrition.
An' Star Wars
Invasions

Bob Marley say
'Until the ignoble and unhappy regimes
That now hold our brothers In Angola
Mozambique, South Africa In subhuman bondage
Have been toppled
Utterly destroyed
Everywhere is war

Di people dem a march
Anti war
Di people dem a march
Anti war, Star

Stars from Hollywood
Not prepared to fight dis ya war, Star

Bush war
Bin Laden war
Dis Sad-damn War, is oil war
Too much war, Star

Bush and Sad Man
Should fight their own war
We should lock them in a war room
An mek dem fight dem war, Star

Di only way to stop all wars
Is to make men
Carry babies for nine months
Leaving dem wid C-section scars
Then man wouldn't be so quick to send dem boys and girls
To fight unnecessary wars, Star

War. War. War.
Mek wi stop dis ya war
Eee, Star?

Lies

TRAVIS BLACKMAN

The problem is you people don't know how to use your heads
If butter gives you heart attacks why do you put it on your bread?
Because you're confused. Even if you could do something, you would be too afraid or too lazy to do it.
If you put a nail in coke it will disintegrate in two days.
Imagine what it's doing to your body, truly. We're living so unruly.
Truthfully it hurts, 'cause we judge someone's appearance and we go sit down in church.
And say how much we like to hear it when the preacher says his words.
It's absurd.   Amalgamation now.
Earth is slaughterhouse, me brown cow, trying to tell other cows about the slaughterhouse.
Before we get chopped up wrapped and ordered out. To be put on a shelf in a store that's 'fresh obsessed'.
Beef isn't naturally red, they dye the flesh. I suggest you enlighten your mind.
Read a good book and see Bowling for Columbine, no lies.
The revolution won't be televised. Read between the lies and then you'll start to get it.
It's called the White House 'cause there's no black people in it.
Which puppet do you choose to carry on your back?
Swollen Colin Powell doesn't qualify as black. Neither does Michael Jackson, neither does Tiger Woods.
Neither does Snow, although he wishes that he could.
They track you down with cell phones people, they're listening.
Roger that, ring a Bell, Telus everything. Motorola, Cantel, Fido fetch and bring.
She sells seashells by the seashore. There's a chemical in tampons that make you bleed more.
So you have to buy more tampons to stop the bleeding.
Am I getting through to you people are you receiving?
Foundation's thick and heavy it makes you pretty of course.
It also clogs the holes in your skin, which are called your pores.
Then you get black heads 'cause the make-up causes zits,
But then to solve the problem they sell you Biore strips.
But those dry out your skin, so they sell you moisture lotion.
And the cycle just continues and you shoppers keep on going out and buying all their product.
They're brainwashing the city.
Make up makes your natural skin ugly, so you have to buy more make up to make your ugly skin pretty.
Don't wallow in self-pity, just wake up to the fact that it's called make up, 'cause the beauty is made up.
How long you gonna take it? I think it's really mean if someone's talkin' 'bout your looks and says maybe
it's Maybelline. Why? Because you're worth it, c'mon it's Nice and Easy.
Oil of Olay twice a day, for sheezy my neezy, squeezy, breezy, beautiful cover girl.
Nice shade, what is that mother of pearl?

Three minutes a day and you can look like Arnold,
Then the next commercial is for Burger King or McDonald's.
Which is only half the reason why the most of you get fat,
But that's okay if most you people out there resent that.
'Cause here to save the day the next commercial is Slim Fast.
And after usin' that, brush your teeth with Colgate.
'Cause if your breath isn't minty then you won't find a soulmate.
And after usin' Colgate, floss three times, and if your gums start to hurt, buy Sensodyne.
Which really does nothing but make your teeth weak. Don't believe me? Go use it and try to eat meat.
And see if your teeth don't start hurtin' ya with size. Lies in the media, lies, lies, lies.
It'll make you cool, it'll make ya smarter, it'll even make you jump like Vince Carter.
It'll make you fit, just like that. But they neglect to mention that the crap'll make ya fat.
It'll make ya black, it'll make ya white. And if ya can't see, it'll give ya sight.
Weed is addictive it kills your brain, you figure.
But Tylenol's addictive and it kills your liver quicker.
Everything on this earth was meant for you to take in.
Too much of anything is bad you must take it in moderation.
But still say no to the medicines grown from the Earth.
Say yes to the ones that are made at work and put on a shelf for you to buy.
You don't even know you're hypnotized.
In the winter time there's salt all around and the salt's all around to melt the ice down.
Then the salt gets wet and absorbed into the ground and leaks into the water.
And kills everyone in the house. Father, son, mother, daughter.
Every summer it gets hotter, global warming's in the air.
Nobody's saying save the ozone layer, cause it isn't there.
But so you don't get scared they say it's regenerating.
Which is a lie cause pollution's constantly penetrating.
Nobody's contemplating a word they say.
Why would they say to save it if they knew it could regenerate?
Then they say save the whales, but you know that they're bluffing.
What have they done for the whales?...absolutely nothing.
And even if there was something they could do.
Why send money to whales, do they send money to you?
I love creatures, I'm not preaching a hunter's tale.
But never in my life have I said to myself:
"This would be so much easier right now if I had myself a nice whale!"
If you wanna save a whale the first thing you should do
Is go to Marine Land and set free Shammu.

Go Shammu go, go Shammu go.
And never come back because they treat you like a ho.
If the speed limit is 60 why make cars that go 250,
And then give me a speeding ticket in a car that's built for racing?
How come successful blacks are mostly athletes and entertainers?
It's a beautiful day, won't you be my neighbour?
What a lifesaver, security systems, that send police to your house, but what if you piss them off?
Suddenly your doors are locked and two minutes later at your door is the cops.
And you're escorted off for speaking your mind, because soon speaking your mind will be a new crime.
And you'll get sentenced five to nine, or nine to life.
And there's nothing you can do 'cause you were paying the toll,
For your house to be completely under someone else's control.
Take a nice little stroll, now it's up to you to look at security systems and figure out what they do.
They protect you, sure, true, maybe it's to secure you.
Cause if you don't do what you're told and you break out of the cycle
Whoops, there goes your heating, whoops, there goes your hydro.
Alert the interceptors a powerful person enters. There's cameras in every one of your fire detectors.
That's why the installation is free, conveniently built into every house and apartment that you see.
With the Internet the world is at your fingertips, but you're also at the fingertips of the world.
Figure it out. Before it's too late to escape. Would you like it if a number were to replace your name?
And every morning when you woke up you were a slave to the state.
But you were young and didn't know your full potential so they invaded your brain.
And programmed it with tonnes of junk not sayin' how it truly works.
Cause it is the most powerful instrument in the universe.
What if every newborn baby must be registered at birth,
And they take each little baby and they estimate their worth?
And how much money you will make in life, so then you'll have to pay them.
And to make sure that it happens they give you free education.
Which really teaches nothing but how to work for somebody else and make them lots of money.
And how to kiss their asses. And if you make what they estimate, they collect it from taxes.
All over the atlas they do it, those little bastards!
Wouldn't it be scary if all those things were to happen?
My name is 12345, not Travis Blackman. Your name is 7 8 9 10, nothin' other.
You are nothing if you don't have a social insurance number.
Just what did they use before this strange number occurred?
Why do I need a number to be socially insured?
Listen to me closely, and you'll see how we have slowly
Been turned into slaves without anybody even knowing.

Objection

FEMI AUSTIN

I beg to differ
With notions of proprietorship
That make my hair fair game
And my body topic worthy

So degraded at times...

Little Suzy Q likens my locks
To monkey fur
So fitting, so ironic
When aped into oblivion in 2004
White folks today
       appear more black than we do
That's black aesthetic
Not black hardship, black disenfranchisement
Or general black bull
Trademarked, stamped and brought to the masses
When Britney Spears
Has the nerve to sing about
Being a 'Slave 4 U'
So now our pain and misery
       can be flipped into something cool
The Neptune's create exploitation's soundtrack
What's this world really coming to?

Makes me wanna say...

Forget Dr. Phil and Oprah
I've got the certified truth
Pink girls have a monopoly on self-esteem
So these 'minor' affronts to your dignity
       are really all about you
Super-sensitive
Chip on your shoulder
Grudge-carrying bitch
Like, that happened so very long ago
Why can't you just get over it?!?!?

But I beg to differ

Especially with co-workers who trust
A simple 'hello' won't do
'wha gwan' with fist extended
too often humouring the humourless
What becomes of this consciousness?
Where black = Jamaican
Though I'm proud of Yard strengthened roots
Taking issue only
With unquestioned rights to assume
And once again become
The honourary black fool
Sambo, darling, entertainer
Be a team player
And make us feel good
Automatically
        voted the authority
On weed, dance moves and rap songs
So objectified
That my objectivity becomes tainted
Appropriated
So disoriented
Mentally dislocated

Please excuse me if I beg to differ.

this is my rant:

NAH-EE-LAH/NAILA K.M. BELVETT

An excerpt from a piece by nah-ee-lah/naila first published in Chimurenga Vol. 3 -Biko in Parliament.

just last night i was reasoning, lime-ing with a bredrin/writer/poet friend discussing how toxic north america is and how imperative it is that we bounce? get the hell out of here as often as possible to maintain/attain some semblance of perspective (yeah? nothing like financial privilege.)

continually bombarbed by propaganda machines. numb. the natural result of excessive north american conditioning. numb. i am. close to being immune too. politics slip so easily. chant down babylon one minute, surf the net to price my future SUV the next – complete with tan leather interior and brown tinted windows (not black – that's far too ghetto.) struggling i am. enticed by the perceived beauty and the lure of that sweet sweet black suburban bourgeoisie.

and what's the alternative? actually live the politics i spew in 'conscious' social circles? damn. all that 'revolution of self' talk makes me nauseous.

conveniently conscious sister. looking for a conveniently conscious significant other so we can sit back, relax and listen to the 8 track – maybe unwind over a bottle of good south african red wine, make love till the sun sets again and revolutionize the world sprawled out on plush leather couches after a delicious three course meal.

i'm saying.

i feel so inadequate. and somewhere inside i know there isn't enough stuff in the world to make me feel better, but I'll probably die before i stop trying to buy my way out of emptiness. sick just thinking about it. lonely. i am. lonely. with no one to invest all of my love energy into. it sucks. u hear me. it sucks.

i don't even know if i have the energy to talk politics. discuss world issues. drop names. show how well read i am. be 'deep' as i navigate my way into the conscious, conscious really conscious black crew. u know, the one that's super critical of most mcees for not keeping it real enough. u know, the crew of readers/thinkers that chant down babylon with proper colonial english sophistication.

well i'm that sista who's tired of trying to fit.   that sista, raised in so much white it seeps out of her pores when she least expects it.   i'm that canadian, trying to be jamaican, african-faking, sista. that creative type writer. singer. actor. actor who's trying to get paid for what she does in everyday life on the regular. that platinum blond wig owning, sweet essential oil wearing, bougie, materialistic, spiritual nigga. the one that doesn't fit. that sister outsider womban? spirit blazing fire shy as hell typa sista. that eyebrow plucking, armpit shaving (on occasion), hairy-legged sista. the one who fluctuates from style to style, from gender to gender, from sanity to other, sista.

so yeah - it's crazy right. cause this world has been ruled by male misogynist energy for so long that the female energy is suspended on the cross and our blood is being shed. with each rape, with each distorted image, with each apology we make for who we be. that female energy, circumcised, manipulated and relegated to the back, so that intellectual debates about black political change can occur.

man. my womb is the change.
call me that angry black bitch sister nigger. birthing the next generation with no support or voice.
suicide. suicide. suicide. hovers on the breath, in the realms of thought of all the so-called strong
black/womyn/warriors
i know.

is there room in the revolution to deal with that?

send blessings, we need them.
from the cold north,

nah-ee-lah

First World Nigger

CHERYL "NNEKA" HAZELL

Say, a chauffeur from the Motherland
Asked me if I was from thither
I smiled half ashamed
"No," I said, "I'm just another first world nigger"

See with your third eye:
        The hat I wore upon my crown trimmed in leopard print may have opened a door, may have
pricked at a sore
which held me hostage since eons past but
my story has been shifted
and tainted
and gutted
and blotted
and de-programmed to best re-program me in this new world.

Say, my roots run deep from where?
        Unknown.
But my Pappy once mentioned a river
And the driver blushed at the notion of
A born and bred first world nigger.

Tune in with your sixth sense:
      And know that long before the shackles and
systemized
polarized
legalized
justified
sanctified
kidnappings and abuse
were the beauty
and glory
and greed
and cunning
and genius
and deceit
and wealth of Civilization. CAPITALIZED.
Original man. CAPITALIZED.
Authentic woman. CAPITALIZED.

Say, I tipped the driver but he pressed me hard to know
if we could talk, you know
Just linger
"Not this time, maybe next."
'Cause right now, kinda vex,
that I'm branded as,
looked upon
spat upon
decidedly dubbed first world nigger

Diaspora
KAMAU

Imagine that you had nothing to gain from change
And even less to gain if the world stayed the same
Imagine you were forced into another man's name
Born into the title of another man's shame
And believed your skin to be a curse and a pain
They hid the fact that you walked this earth first
Stole the claim of a proud people

My worth never was considered equal
Considered ignorant, thieving and feeble
Imagine you heard the verses and internalized their belief systems
Imagine they stole all the lives that you could give them
And gave you little back
They allowed you to laugh
And you felt that you were free
Trapped your past in the past
I welcome you to the present

Although it's obvious who lacks the power and who remains dominant
I still speak although I often feel weak
I pray the ancestors rest well in their sleep
This isn't my world
This isn't my world
This isn't my world
This never has been my world

They pressed our baby girls curls and told her she was now beautiful, at long last
She wished for her skin to be a part of their caste
But what about you?
What about the beauty of you?
What about us?
Diamonds are our daughters of dust
To dust and ashes they burnt us alive
Some hung from trees like autumn just for us to survive
And they asked us to forget and too many of us did

And we never spoke about it and chose not to teach our kids
But what now? Their world closes around us
Chains on our feet saw the seas deep, they drowned us
Without a second thought
Abandoned our humanity it's like we never fought
To alleviate the tragedy

Now we see ourselves only through their eyes
And live our lives in the shadows of their lies
I was taught in his schools, raised in his community
Appropriation and assimilation is his unity
But what about us?
God, what about us?
What about us?
Even our own sons we distrust, we're one and the same
All we do is try to place ourselves inside of their petty game
But few of us know from where we came
So much confusion, where do we place the blame?
Some of them ask me why I'm angry
But what I am is tired
Tired of having to fight for the freedom we've desired
For so many years
So many tears
Rolled down the cheeks of our black faces in fear

Heartache and pain standing over the graves
Of our forefathers who were descended from slaves
I'm tired of reacting I just want to live
But we have nowhere to call our own
So little left to give
Where do we place the blame?
How do we stay the same?
Funny how we still call each other the same names
That they used to keep us down
It's like we love the sound
Of insults the result is the word is still around
Loud and out in the open, so many hearts we've broken
Because this simple ignorance continues to be spoken

Remember how they raped us
No matter how they paint us
With love on our side they could barely stand against us
Still they forced us to the ground, claimed that we were savages
Tore us from our tradition
Desecrated our languages

How is it we can regain power and prominence
When my people are separated and scattered across the continents?
While they reap the benefits of a people's free labour
Claiming no responsibility generations later
We've built many a nation almost from their birth
It's no coincidence that they're the strongest countries on the earth
Begging for some peace
Our spirits in the East
Served and protected and seen as guilty by police
These days it seems it doesn't even matter what we say
Being forced into new struggles every living day
Search for truth and you will find it
Some have to be reminded
Of the struggle we continue to go through no longer blinded
By what we need to communicate
We are not alone
We're all trapped in the Diaspora and looking for a home

"Stylistically my work reflects a longing like one in exile, a romantic nostalgic quest to return home to one's roots."
– Melville White, author Love Rhapsodies and Blues.

First Generation Ethiopian/Canadian
WEYNI MENGESHA

I have left long ago with the likeness of my youthful return
I left with the history and colours of my people
The voices of my mothers and fathers
The God in my house and the kneeling fruit of my country
I left the sun rising from the Red Sea upon the pepper trees
Dancing shoulders and necks that slide to the laughter of the drums

The sweet air and dusty roads that lined my body with the protection
Excluding the intruder
Knotting in their throats
Alarming us of their presence

The fertile ground that stood upon the shoulders of generations beneath us
I left with its root in my belly to build castles for her in a new promised land

I have journeyed
I lay my back on cold strange ground
Knees towards the sky
As the Red Sea carries her out between my legs and she is new
No longer inside of me
To feed from the songs and stories that my body carries

I have forgotten now
I am now my daughter

Many years my mother has left behind to build castles for me in this promised land
I cannot remember what she tries to tell me with her eyes of mine of centuries
As I return with the likeness of her youth
I fight to remember

I step down off the plane
The earth in my body trembles with confusion
There are whispers in the dusty wind that tickle in my throat
Trying to discover me
I taste the honey and milk of my mother's tongue but it sticks and branches in my mouth
The faces around me smile and stretch with the voices and hands
My mothers' faces greet me
Showering me in a raining melody of "ELELELELEL"

I hear it drum a pace just beside my heartbeat
A resounding sound that opens me
Unconscious
A moment in time
I am the daughter and my mother has let me go
I walk alone with her face
And her soul is still to be known

There's a Reason My Patois's Not So Good

STEVEN GREEN

steel bird touches rubber to ground
through the roundabout in a JUTA taxi
and through the window
I eyeball everything:

bush on walls coming through cracks
crawling up
to big houses stacked and staggered
sprawling out on the few flat stretches of land before the poor can get there
shaken up and scattered like dice
tumbled into place out of a colonial hiccup or deep belly cough
blisters on landscapes grafted against land that knows better where people do not
my wide eyes struggle to say what my mouth cannot
because my patois's not so good
trying to swallow my claim to the third world

a poorly tuned car whines and mangy dog yelps
this is jamaica buddy
and there's a reason my patois's not so good
ribs exposed dog, belly like children hungry
black kids soft feet play in hard street with no shoes among
shanty town buildings jumbled up and shook down and laid out in PNP and JLP stepping stones
How do you feel now about where you should be from?

and there's a reason my patois's not so good:
on the way over oxford got mixed in with labrish* and guess what got sifted out by the cultural sieve
of north american public schools?
blowing softly on the sands of my syntax and flutters and tattoos like plagues peeling off the edges of
my own infinite white space
where I learned to make love
naked and peeled to the pink
where I learned to make love
inside that white space I saw as a reflection of me
it comforted me and
I learned to make love

which of course now I will defend from each returning grain
I will defend with a shield metal colander
I will descend to the "New World" with a fish net parachute
Of course I will defend against rushing brown dirt
and broken cars
broken buildings
broken English
the sands rushing back to my address which my gravity may have moved but has not changed
threatening to remind me and those I make
tender
pink
alien love to that I am a foreign object
an erect obelisk
not
pink
quivering
flesh
threatening to set me outside of infinite white space
a philosophy I cannot comprehend
existing outside of infinite white space?
nothing
but rushing black sand

West Indian colloquiallism for talk or conversation

a dollar

NAH-EE-LAH/NAILA BELVETT

can't handle cry freedom
steven biko or his pain
prefer to watch kung fu flicks
than see the depths of subconscious tricks
instilled within the black mind
raping the innocence of every black baby it can find

the soul of democracy's hypocrisy lives on
but not my master's hand
see the clever master plan
only needed a few licks from massa stick
to be imbedded in the black soul for more than a lifetime
the fear to be passed along for generations
along the life line

nurtured in, by, through us it would grow – prosper
seed planted in the womb of the house negress
an alternative lay later promoted to mistress
inbreeded, half-breeded, confused mulatto she was mixed
but searching for pride refused to mix with the field niggas in the yard
erecting barriers of good hair, straight nose, slightly narrower hips
boasting a high yellow complexion while sucking in her thick bottom lip
distancing herself from her self reflected in the field niggers in the yard
centuries later our 'niggas' feel up their 'bitches' in elementary school yards
enslaved by complexes of inferiority
confused by the difference between their reality
and the one lived by the white minority called society

and now i hold a dollar in my hand
convinced that with it i can buy me a new master plan
then i bring my dollar to the bank and find out that in this world
it's only worth two quarters and a dime
sixty cents calculated after the u.s. exchange rate
but my canadian paycheck didn't compensate for the difference
it never added a quarter, a nickel, a dime
forty more cents so a dollar could make sense and be a dollar

but i really just hold a dollar full up of nonsense
cause it's really just two quarters and ten cents
then i checked the paycheque
did a double check
realized after taxes
sixty cents was demoted to a dime
i need some time to figure out
who benefits from this hypocritical, american dreaming
deflated by canadian currency
i feel a sense of urgency

physically free while mentally imprisoned
i'm starting to lose my vision
i wanted to buy in
pretend like no struggle i'm in
with two eyes open
(and a third one closed)
i could live out a happy existence
marry white, two kids, a pathfinder - maybe a jeep
a johnson family name plate on our front door to greet
our neighbours
but none of them would be sisters or brothers
hell and risk having my property value decrease?
naw
instead i would choose to increase my ignorance
and turn my back on all the others
that look like me
that looked like me
                                    ...that is me

afraid to hear the truths about my people
yet living proof of the truths of my people
don't want to read no books or see no films about my people
yet living a flick of my own with every click of the father clock
that statistics show could be cut short by the click of a black brothers glock

and still i hold this dollar in my hand
well in fact it's just a dime
but i was hoping with it i could just a little more time

see i thought it would make me part of society
with it i had plans to buy more nike
i thought i behind it i could mask all my insecurites
forgot my aunty was the house nigress
forgot my sister was massa's mistress
forgot my mommy was the white babies mammy
forgot my granny breastfed the same babies
that went on to whip her grand babies
forget my father was kunta kinte
and now i wonder why i limp in modern day society

and i wonder why
i'm holding fast to this dime
when i feel like running out from under me is time
can't watch cry freedom biko's life too close to home
but i ball crying for freedom every night when i'm alone

if i could just undo history
if i could just take back centuries
or if god had just asked me
when my spirit sat in heaven
waiting to be born
with which physical traits i wanted it to be born
than i could have evaluated the situation and picked
white - so i could live right

so my dollar could be the dollar
so my dream could be society's reality
so my heaven could be right here on earth
so my children wouldn't have to struggle or fight for identity
for equality
for the right to be

once a dollar
now a dime
on my knees
i pray to god
for a little more
time.

Pause

JEDDIAH ISHMEL

I'm 26 years old and I got no kids
As a little boy I was taught to handle my biz
So I did a little school and y'all know how that is
But now I got a little job and my story begins
My little aspiration was a big paycheque
With a little determination earned a little bit of respect
With a little bit of respect came a little bit of success
And with a little bit of success came nuff stress

Now nuff stress is going to drive your butt nutty
My back is full of knots, my head is full of putty
I take my every hour and sell the 24
Now I'm taking campaign contributions to lobby for more
If you gave me 25 I'd use it for sleep
If you gave me 26 I'd make food to eat
If you gave me 27 I'd call my friends back
28 would be great I could avoid a heart attack
Get that social life I lack
Or just sit back ...
Write a poem, draw a picture or record a dancehall track
In fact, I could smell the roses I could obey the road laws
I could... I could... I could...

Pause

I'm 26 years old and I got no kids
I can't help but wonder what would happen if I did
Would they recognize my face, or even know my name
Would they say Easter Bunny, Tooth Fairy, Daddy all the same?
He comes around once a year, brings nuff gear
Mommy's probably joking, but she says he lives here
Am I to become a spook?
Call me spook squared
Running scared from my kids that never knew I cared
I could hug my bank account and play Daddy Santa Clause
Or I could... I could ... I could...

Pause

I'd like to take this break to say...
Sorry,
But I have no more time
Because I gave all of mine
To some cold and heartless company
That swallowed up and spat out me
I'm sorry, I'm sorry

Forgive me
I'm 26 years old and I work at a desk
I pause just to breathe
I pause for the stress
I pause for the cause no matter what it is
I pause to think about my unborn kids
I pause to write a poem
I pause for a cup of coffee
I don't drink the stuff but I won't let that stop me
I could get three or four more pauses if I were to take up smoking
I pause to think about it, pause 'cause I'm joking
I pause to bust a five line email out to a friend
I have to pause from my pauses to get some work done in the end
As I pause to ponder how I live through my pause control
Stealing back my life from the hours that I sold
I pause...

I'm 26 years old and I got no kids
As a little boy I was taught to handle my biz
To handle my biz is to put my life in order
Weigh my dreams and their costs to make sure I can afford to
Pause...

Black Like Me
hERONJONSE

One, 2... 1, Two...
Yo, I'm chocolate like a bar
Far from a Caucasian
My skin has a pigment reminiscent of a tan and I
Plan to grow dreads, but first this nappy fro
The coils in my hair contain potential energy, you didn't know

I remember when I was young
Black wasn't the cool thing to be
But once I reached high school it seemed that every culture wanted to be like me
Even the black kids who acted more like white kids
Were following the white kids who were now acting more like black kids
And for the white kids who chose not to assimilate
Their biggest complaint was that the black students never spoke patois back in grade eight

In grades three and four I led a gang war against the Italians
In my neighborhood of Downsview
For weeks at a time every recess we'd put up our dukes, later call a truce
Until one offended the other again during classes at elementary school
From Jane and Finch I moved to Brampton
In the lining of my jacket I carried a weapon called a skinhead beater
For the white kids who wore white laces in their black Doc Martin's
To symbolize their racist behavior

High school, only dark skinned kids dare hang out in the student area
It was known even to other schools as Central Africa
Until the principal decided to rip it out
Said it was a distraction to the classes
But all the black students knew what it was really about

I remember it had to be a special occasion
When the after school black history class was well attended
One time a student declared that the first human being was black
And the whole class was in disbelief
Until it was confirmed by the white teach

I think b(l)ack to the first time being stopped by the beast
Cops clutching their guns
Saying that me and my young friends fit the description of midnight thieves

I remember moving into a new house, the one next door was still under construction
When the workers left for the evening
Some neighborhood white kids were playing with the machines
Next morning a worker asked me who done it. But I ain't no snitch yo
His response was, why all you black bastards always saying I don't know

I remember when I once thought Jesus was white
I've since deprogrammed my mind but sometimes, I still struggle to get the picture right
I went to a predominantly black church
But when we held conferences with affiliating assemblies it seemed
That the white breddrin were always considered the bible experts

When I think back in time my closest white friend in junior high was jealous of me
Taught me how to play basketball still I was better naturally
From the comments would make under his breath
I could tell he was racist
But like Mike, Magic, and Dominique he wanted to be
Hate us and revere us it's the same old story

And then I remember when rap music was... black music
And the white kids who were down were considered wannabees
Yo, I remember telling a teacher that I was going on vacation
To my parent's home in the Caribbean
And his assumption was that Jamaica was the only island in the West Indies

One, 2... 1, Two
I ain't even going as far as to say three
Before I finish recollecting
This goes out to everyone who has any recollection
Of being black like me

Children of the Sun

hERONJONSE

We people, children of the sun
Called burnt faces
Revered by every...
Loved by none

We people, children of the sun
The first to be suspected, placed on the front line
The first to be created
The so called missing link, last kink in the time line

Accused of being too sexual
Aroused by the rays of passion
Melanin photosynthesis, our epidermis, like fossil fuels
Share love affairs with the flame's affection

We're right brain inclined
Intuitive by nature
Excelling in sports, arts
And any business that's of a spiritual nature

With ease we surf on rhythms
And wine our waists on candlewicks
Our whole being, like the Earth
Is a duplicate of the Creator's myriad of images

We people, children of the sun
Lovers of light, which is why some
Of our cold-blooded youth fiend for the beams of a buzz
And are so quick to flash jewels, white crystals and guns

Running relay races on rainbows chasing the glimmer of gold
Who could have imagined that our tropical hearts could turn so cold?
Who could have dreamed that the legacy of our lives
Could become a substance to be stole?

So many wander through the night
Like onyx stones skipping through dark waters
With a flickering shine
That quickly fades with time

Some wait patiently
And pray for the bright light of tomorrow
While others ignite fires
By striking matches against their pain, anger and sorrow

Still we're thankful for the moon
The mirror which reveals the sun's reflection
It exposes our glittering relatives
Who stand on guard for our protection

So we people, children of the sun
Continue to look towards the light, for our day is soon to come
The clouds will cushion us as we dive into that celestial abyss
To be reunited in the womb with our family's glowing spirit

So don't give up don't give in sun's children
We may have to begin again from the beginning
To feel the warmth of heaven
We may have to begin again from our glorious beginning
To feel the warmth of heaven

Water Carrier

MEL WHITE

We the people of the golden
Shimmering sun
Carry the world on our head
And it's shame on our scarred back
Balancing it with love in our sacred heart
Moving ahead with pride
Poised on the brink of a
Brighter tomorrow
We waltz toward a
Glorious future
Filled
With
Hope

"The audience for my work is humanity. Everyone can learn something new."
– Sankofa, Host, Urban Griots (105.5 FM)

A *Foothold In The Snow*

AFTERWORD by KAREN RICHARDSON

After completing my undergraduate studies as McGill University, I returned to Toronto eager to participate in the burgeoning arts community. Armed with a collection of new poems written over my four years in Montreal, I was ready to find a stage on which to share in the place I knew best. Perhaps, I would walk through the Arrivals door at Pearson Airport's terminal three and a host of promoters and respected literati would be bidding for the privilege to chauffeur me to my next gig. Not so.

The winter was cold that year. The city began to cocoon itself safely into its artistic ghettos and I, the returning ex-patriot nostalgic for home, was homeless. Did I remember incorrectly? Weren't there several of places to perform? Why couldn't I fit in? The self-inflicted performance hiatus to ensue would last about six months. I would not fight my way into what I considered to be the existing cliques. Toronto is a city replete with peoples of all nations and tongues, value systems and vantage points. Why should I, after finally identifying my unique artistic voice, shove this square peg anywhere apart from the square hole predestined for me? My job then was to find it.

In a multiethnic city, plurality dulls the intensity of a single voice. The power of one community is further quenched by duplicity within. United together, our cries for justice may be heard and our prayers for recognition answered. As I reconnected with the city of my childhood, I met countless others who agreed it was time to deliberately cause artists in Toronto, particularly black artists, to act as one unified community. We needed a meeting place. We required a system whereby we could share our views via the art we produced. We needed to shatter the walls between us in order to mutually benefit from the increasing demand on our creativity, so we created La Parole.

Dubbed 'Toronto's Speech Therapy for the Creative Mind', La Parole has encouraged artists and audiences to speak to each other since June of 2002. Tucked away on the third floor of Flava Restaurant on Yonge St, the interactive weekly showcase is the training ground for a new generation of community-centred artists. It is the non-partisan environment wherein cliques are penetrated and uncensored dialogue is its essence. Poets mingle with playwrights, actors with photographers, painters with storytellers and producers with musicians. It was in that setting where T-Dot Griots was born.

Only two months after the event got started, the idea to produce this anthology firmly took root in the minds of Steven Green and myself. We were overwhelmed by Toronto's well known writers and performers as well as a bevy of newcomers, all equally excited to have a regular meeting place to share their work and ideas. No one to impress. No hurdles to jump. Unhindered access to an audience of their peers. These storytellers walk Toronto's streets and all experience life in the city through unique pairs of eyes. Every Friday we enjoy the chance to hear these stories freshly related to whomever would listen.

T-Dot Griots is a literary meeting place for such artists. Canonized here, our words shall live on to document our experience in this land of migrants called Canada. The anthology is one step in a multigenerational process to inform existing communities of our presence. We are Toronto's black storytellers; standing together in hopes that the world might see us, Africans in a foreign land where transplanted roots fight for a foothold in the snow.

This winter I am hopeful. I look forward to embracing fellow artists and friends. I am warmed by the fire in their words, soothed by the heat of their voices. From the Bluffs to the Caledon Hills, the Pickering power plant to Sky Dome, right up to the Maraine, my words find residence. I hear the crackling syllables on open stages and I know something is happening. Our words live here and in case you haven't noticed – so do we.

Thank you for reading our stories.

Contributors

Unblind Africanus

Unblind Africanus is an African divinist, poet, griot and scribe. He was born in Africa and migrated to Europe with his family at age six. Unblind remained in Switzerland and England before arriving in Toronto. After graduating with Master's in Economics, he decided to answer his life calling and become a poet. Since then he has performed at Afrofest, Planet Africa (Toronto International Film Festival), Marcus Garvey Day Celebrations, Malcolm X Day Commemoration and Vibe. Unblind is the author of a self-titled, self-published book and a live CD entitled *"Unblind Uncut-live from the T-dot."*

Jesse Andrews

Trinidad-native Jesse Andrews produced a one-hour video entitled *"Pan Secrets"* on how to play the tenor pan. The following year he released a design for the tenor pan watch face. Jesse's first book of pan poetry is entitled *"Crackshot Pan Poems"* in which he coined the phrase "port of pan" referring to Port of Spain, Trinidad and Tobago in the poem Voice from a Manager, Port of Pan. In 1997 he published two more books of pan poetry; *Pan Soul Vibrations Pan Poems* and *Bareback Pan Sticks Pan Poems.* Jesse is also a high-jumper, having represented Canada in Barcelona, Spain in 2003

Trey Anthony

Trained in the Performing Arts Program at George Brown College, Trey Anthony, owner of Plaitform Entertainment is an actor, playwright and comedian. As a comic, Trey has performed at Yuk Yuk's at Second City. On television, she has appeared on the Chris Rock Show and WTN. Although best known for her hilarious sketch characters, Anthony chose the vehicle of theatre to deliver intimate personal experiences. Her first play *'da kink in my hair* drew sold out audiences for each of its runs.

Femi Austin

Femi Austin explores the nature of struggle in her work. She examines how struggle is informed by our history, present and future. The word is power and through our truths we derive strength and clarity. From acting a as a literacy tutor to researching the pyscho-social factors contributing to depression in young women, Femi remains optimistic that creative solutions can be developed to confront some of our greatest challenges. Her writing is an effort to articulate and challenge the inevitability of struggle. Femi holds a degree from the University of Toronto and is currently pursuing a degree in Law from Rutgers University in New Jersey.

Travis A. Blackman

Travis A. Blackman is the 2003 champion of the Up From the Roots International Poetry Slam. With rhymes addressing genetic engineering, intoxication, nanotechnology, the apocalypse, violence, hypocrisy, self empowerment, spirituality, and awareness Blackman is fast becoming a crowd favourite. His work is satirical using catchy pop-culture references and cliché to highlight inconsistencies in western culture. Whether delivering long hip-hop influenced rants or projecting his bellowing voice to fill a room with dub-inspired chants, Travis gives a memorable live performance that will leave each listener deep in thought.

Sandra Brewster

Using various media on canvas and paper Sandra Brewster visually depicts narratives exploring representation. Through portraiture she focuses on Canadians whose identities are formed in Canada, but whose roots lie elsewhere. Exhibitions include: Through My Eyes, Through My Spirit, with Natalie Wood and Jacqueline Ward (Spadina Historic House and Gardens), Thupelo, (South African National Gallery, Cape Town, South Africa), Last Stop, (St. Norbert's Arts Centre, St. Norbert, Manitoba) and in October 2002 she held a solo exhibiton at Zsa Zsa (Queen Street West gallery strip, Toronto). Sandra is a graduate of York University with a Bachelors of Fine Arts.

Wakefield Brewster

Dynamic, prolific, and all about being a spoken word artist. Beginning with open stages, Brewster is at home as a featured guest at festivals, readings and fundraisers. Brewster is a repeat act at British Columbia's Shambhala Festival, performing for an audience of 8,000. He is just as happy in the intimate setting of his Pitbull Poetry Reading Series, held monthly in lounges and bars across Toronto. Brewster now gives lectures at York University on spoken word, expression and political science.

Wakefield has performed at many venues including Nuyorican Poet's Café, New York City, and TIO The Merriment of Ten and the Children's Wish Foundation in Toronto.

Ernest Carter*

Originally from the United States, Ernest Carter is a visual artist and poet. He has performed around the city at such events as Café Che, The Pitbull Poetry Series, and Mix it Up and Take it Down, a monthly open mic night in support of OCAP (Ontario Coalition Against Poverty). He is currently instructing art classes for children and organizing art shows around the city. Ernest currently lives in Toronto where he is raising his five year old daughter.

Jacqueline Cohen

Jacqueline Cohen is the Excutive Director of the Power of Expression Art Auction, founder of the Our Image Visual Arts Awards and owner of Our Image Greeting Cards. The art auction has featured the works of black Canadian artists since 1997. To date approximately $80,000 in art has been in this forum. The awards are uniquely designated to acknowledge the great work of artists of African descent in Canada. Cohen's Toronto-based company specializes in cultural greeting cards and art products.

Afua Cooper

Dr. Afua Cooper is a writer of non-fiction, history and poetry. She holds a Ph.D. in African-Canadian history with specialties in slavery and abolition. She has expertise in women's history and New France studies, contributing to several publications on the history of the African Diaspora in Canada and the Caribbean. She teaches history and women's studies at York and Ryerson universities. As a pioneer in dub poetry, she helped establish its roots in Canada. Her works include *Memories Have Tongue, Utterances and Incantations: Women, Poetry and Dub* (with co-editors Peggy Bristow and Dionne Brand) and *We're Rooted Here and They Can't Pull Us Up: Essays in African Canadian Women's History.*

Del F. Cowie

Del F. Cowie is a freelance writer based in Toronto, Canada. He has written about hip-hop music and culture for US publications Vibe and URB. In Toronto his work has appeared in Eye and Exclaim! where he has served as a Contributing Editor.

Eddy David/Da Original One*

Eddy David was raised in Ottawa and Trinidad, before making his home in Toronto. The 2001 jury member for the Canada Arts Council spoken word program has opened for the Caribbean comedians Paul Keens-Douglas and Oliver Samuels and folk singer Faith Nolan. He is a storyteller and beat-boxer who uses humour and insight to address socio-political and romantic themes. First published by MACPRI international, Eddy is the former artistic director of Young Poets of the Revolution, Ottawa Chapter. He is featured on *WordlIfe: Tales of the Underground Griots* and has performed in Canada, the United States and the Caribbean.

R. Osaze Dolabaille*

R. Osaze Dolabaille is a committed father, poet, drummer and singer whose goal is to instill a Pan-African sense of identity in his audiences. A Canadian of Trinidadian parentage, Osaze maintains there is no such thing as a Diasporic African community, rather black people in Canada are merely Africans who are living abroad. Osaze got his start performing with Through the Seasons, a group that still initiates performance around Toronto. As a promoter, he has worked together with Naila Chauncey and So Dayi Production to organize gatherings including The Awakening (Caliban Arts Theatre) and Soul Speak (The Faubourg).

Tricia Douglas

Jamaica-born Tricia Douglas immigrated to Toronto at age seven. Holding a degree in Mass Communications and Sociology from York University and a diploma in Journalism from Humber College, Douglas has worked as a professional photographer for six years. Focusing on architecture, people and nature, her photographic work is published in Network (the Canadian Association of Black Journalists newsletter), the Power of Expression Art Auction magazine and on the web. She has participated in This Woman's Work (July 2002) and the Distillery Art Exhibit. Tricia has contributed articles to the Humber Etc. newspaper, the North American Gleaner and Weekly Star and Marlo Magazine. tdphoto@hotmail.com

Jael Ealey

Jael Ealey is a Graduate of the University of Guelph School of Drama. The young playwright completed her first full length piece under the tutelage of Governor-General Award winning playwright Judith Thompson. The play, *My Upside-Down Black Face*, is the story of one black woman's quest to connect and affirm her identity by examining suppressed images and feelings of subjugation and exclusion. It is her journey to discover what being black means to her.

Elicser (cover)

Elicser decorates the city of Toronto with graffiti murals covering the south-western quadrant of the downtown core. He was raised in St. Vincent and the Grenadines before relocating to Toronto at age fifteen. Grandson of novelist G C H Thomas (*Ruler in Hiroona*), Elicser authored a comic strip in the weekly Vincentian newspaper. He is a trained illustrator. From flyers to skateboards, canvas to walls, Elicser lives in the world of images.

Zetta Elliott

Toronto born Zetta Elliott, has lived, studied and taught in the United States since 1994. She considers herself a "commuter;" returning to Toronto three or four times per year and in 1999 spent six months living downtown finishing her first novel. She received her PhD in American Studies from New York University in January, 2003. Much of Zetta's writing focuses on black women's experiences with and resistance to violence. She has written numerous stories for children, while poetry and a performance piece are underway. Zetta is currently researching and writing an historical young adult novel on the New York City Draft Riots of 1863.

Steven Green

(See About the Editors, pg #180)

Jaicyea Hamilton-Smith

Jaicyea Hamilton-Smith is 9 years old and loves to listen to, write and read poetry. At seven years of age she began writing and reciting her poems at the weekly La Parole event held at Flava Restaurant. After listening to other poets she became inspired and began to write. Her contribution to this anthology was written after an incident involving racism occurred at school. She was hurt and wanted to know if there was something wrong with being black. Jaicyea will continue to write and recite poetry due to the sheer satisfaction of expressing herself.

Seth-Adrian Harris

Seth-Adrian Harris is a published author and award winning filmmaker born in Kingston, Jamaica in 1971. In 1976 Seth-Adrian immigrated to Toronto. His work has been called "visceral manifestos of the black experience". Most of his documentaries present the peculiar perspectives and predicaments of immigrants in Canada as "we are often like fish out of water." He is a freelance writer for the Canadian Broadcasting Corporation and has taught film and video production at secondary and post secondary institutions. He currently sits on the boards of various arts foundations in Toronto while pursuing his PhD in Media Studies at Ryerson University.

Cheryl "Nneka" Hazell*

Cheryl Hazell is a Toronto based freelance urban culture writer, editor and performance poet who is following her spirit wherever it may lead. Music is her driving force and the written word her lifeblood. Nneka, her chosen name, is from the Igbo of Nigeria and has a dual meaning: 'woman of purpose' and 'mother is supreme'. Writing can articulate deep-rooted needs, recover passion, and nourish the spirit. Nneka is on a creative journey, on an ongoing mission to find, know and love herself via a unique voice. Equally important to her is the training of her three children.

Nadia L. Hohn

Nadia L. Hohn is a teacher, artist and founder of ICED IN BLACK: Canadian Black Experiences on Film. As a Canadian-born black woman of Jamaican desent, she felt that mainstream media did not acknowledge or portray her unique identity. Her love for education, the arts and black culture all went into the development of ICED IN BLACK. She holds a Honour's Bachelor of Arts degree in Psychology from the University of Waterloo and a Bachelor of Education from the University of Toronto. Currently, she is working towards a graduate degree in Education also at the U of T. www.icedinblack.ca

Jeddiah Ishmel*

Trained at the University of Toronto as an engineer, Jed works in the finance industry. Jed is the first child of immigrants from St. Vincent and the Grenadines. Drawing on their momentum, his drive is paired with a creative energy through his hectic corporate routine and his artistic pursuits. He describes his poetry as a release valve for the inconsistencies he sees in his life; such as financial aspirations versus antiestablishment values or his Christian faith against a sinful life. Jed uses hip-hop influenced rhythm and r-hyme to communicate stories of struggle; consumer friendly packaging for personal trials.

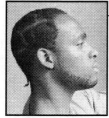

heronJonse dat sweet addiction*

heronJonse is an author and spoken word artist. He self-published a poetry chapbook and completed a live spoken word CD called *Accapella Rhymes*. His goal is to 'edu-tain' audiences. His poetry is a gut-wrenching reminder of the everyday addictions we deny. heronJonse is the Toronto Poetry Slam champion for 2001 and 2003. The former guest on CTV's TalkTV and Raptor's TV's Basketball City was nominated for an Urban Music Association of Canada (UMAC) award for his first CD, *I Love Love but I Hate Valentines Day*. As a journalist, he writes for Ambassador Magazine and (YTM) Your Time magazine and literature reviews for Knowledge Bookstore.

Sankofa Juba

Jamaican born Sankofa has been supporting community initiatives as the host of Urban Griots(CHRY 105.5 FM). A founding member of the arts collective, the West Side Cipher, Sankofa contributes his direct, off-the-cuff dub poetical styles to educate the black community in Toronto about their roots. Sankofa is Akan for 'go back and find it'. Working closely with the Jamaican Canadian Centre and various other groups, Sankofa commits himself to tracing his African heritage and remembering our collective legacy. Sankofa organizes many community oriented events and fundraising initiatives throughout Toronto.

Hajile Kalaike a.k.a. Lotus*

Originally from Maryland, Toronto's "love poet" Hajile Kalaike is known for his smooth and jazzy renditions of inspiring prose. Hajile strives to excel in the poetic arts by reaching as many listeners and readers as possible. He cites Malcolm X (El-Hajj Malik El Shabazz) and John William Coltrane as two major influences, calling them "spiritual fathers". After performing for over seven years and participating in countless community workshops and talent nights in Toronto and in the United States, Hajile's peaceful approach and positivity is revolutionary, progressive, thoughtful and melodious. Hajile specializes in poetry about Life: love, erotica, relationships, community and spiritual enlightenment.

Kathleen Judith James a.k.a. Strong*

Kathleen Judith James graduated from York University concurrent Education and History. She is currently pursuing a Master's degree at Queen University in African-Canadian Studies. Since January 2002, she has written over one hundred poems spanning the issues of love, black history and self-empowerment. Her poetry is published in an academic journal.

Kamau

Kamau, meaning quiet warrior, is the Canadian-born son of Trinidadian filmmakers Claire Prieto and Roger McTair. The poet, lyricist and music producer developed a strong respect for the arts at an early age. Kamau has toured across Canada performing hip-hop and spoken word with Juno and Source award winner K-OS. He released his debut hip-hop EP First in 2003. His involvement in hip-hop music and spoken word stems from the potential he sees in both forms to open the eyes of the youth. Kamau is the founder of the Creation Company and is currently completing his studies in graphic design.

Jason Humphreys Kinte

Jason Humphreys Kinte is a prize-winning motivational speaker, and CEO of Phree Shares Inc. He was born in Toronto of Antiguan parents. His debut CD *Poetry is my Wife* features thirty of his best poems. In 2002, Jason Kinte put his education and experience in the technology and business fields to good use. He established www.torontopoets.com to help poets expose their art. In 2003 he began work on the Increase the Peace campaign to reduce levels of violence in Toronto and around the world.

Malik I.M.

Malik I.M. (Sean C. Isaacs) is a spoken word artist. His poetry and prose writing encompass Diasporic African history, counter-racist education, sociology and social/political commentary to address the forces that affect African peoples both in the Diaspora and on the continent. Malik I.M.'s artistic influences include Saul Williams, Rakim, Sonia Sanchez, Afua Cooper and Mutaburuka for their radical/avant-garde approaches to the griot tradition. Fueled by such passion, Malik I.M. is associated with Black Youth United (BYU), a grassroots reparations organization in the Toronto area. He is trained in social justice and education as a high school teacher.

Yannick Marshall*

Yannick Giovanni Marshall is a 19-year-old poet born in Toronto to a Jamaican mother and St. Lucian father. He spent two years of his childhood in St. Lucia and two years of his adolescence in Botswana, Africa. Both locations influenced much of his descriptive poetry. Together with Nigerian poet Ooto Jones, Yannick is fathering a restoration movement called the Black Redemption Movement. The two co-published a chapbook entitled *Old Friend, We Made This for You* in 2003. Yannick has studied African cultures and poetry independently and is currently pursuing a Bachelor of Arts degree in Political Science at the University of Toronto.

Weyni Mengesha

Vancouver-born, Toronto-raised Weyni Mengesha is Ethiopian/Canadian. She works in theatre in Toronto, primarily as a director with further experience in Vancouver and Halifax. Recent projects include: Assistant Director on the television series *Lord Have Mercy*, director of *da kink in my hair* by Trey Anthony (Theatre Passe Muraille), *3 parts harmony* by Raven Dauda and Ngozi Paul (rock.paper.sistaz), *yagayah* by d'bi.young and nah-ee-lah/naila belvett (Black Theatre Workshop, Montreal and the Africanadian Playwrights Festival), *blood* by d'bi.young (NewYork Hip Hop Theatre Festival). Working with words, music and choreography, she enjoys the ability of theatre to weave community experiences into the fabric of black Canadian culture.

Dwayne Morgan

Dwayne Morgan has been performing his spoken word poetry in Toronto and throughout the world since 1993. He is the founder of Up From The Roots Entertainment. At age twenty-nine, Dwayne has become one of the youngest members of the Canadian League of Poets. Dwayne has shared the stage with Kardinal Offishall, Choclair, Jully Black, K-OS and Saukrates. He has released two spoken word albums: *The Evolution* which received Album of the Year accolades from The Caribbean Camera, and *Soul Searching* for which Dwayne took home his second Urban Music Award for Best Spoken Word Recording. www.upfromtheroots.ca

Maki Motapanyane*

Maki Motapanyane is a Sowetan woman of mixed race, now a Canadian residing in Toronto. The graduate student of York University considers her poetry to be a paper reflection of her ongoing thinking, sorting, struggling and dialoging through the many facets of 'racialization' and all the oppressions that flow with it (gender, class, sexuality, etc.). She is exploring community, transparency, identity, honesty, responsibility and accountability, compassion, self-love and the roles these can/do play in healing black communities and bodies.

Motion

Motion is an emcee, poet and author. Her debut collection, *Motion In Poetry*, was nominated for the ForeWord Magazine book of the year. She is heard on *WordLife: Tales of the Underground Griots, Urbnet's Hip Hop Vol. 2* and Phem Phat's *Honey Drops*. Her releases on Blacklist Music have been played on FLOW 93.5, Much Music and Vibe. As host of CIUT 89.5's "Masterplan Show," Motion won an Urban Music Association award. Motion is the inaugural winner of the CBC National Poetry Face-Off. *Motion In*

Poetry : The AudioXperience is a powerful package of gritty live performances, spoken verse and pulsing lyrics, serving up a flowetic sound feast for the senses. www.motionlive.com.

Jane Musoke-Nteyafas

Jane Musoke-Nteyafas was born in Russia. She has lived in Russia, France, Denmark, Cuba, Uganda and Canada, having traveled extensively throughout the world. She speaks English, French, Spanish, Danish and Luganda. She writes poetry, lyrics and short stories and is currently working on publishing her first book *Daughters of the Earth*. "Poetry and art are my passions. I am proud of my African roots and my poetry reflects that," says Jane. She is a visual artist, specializing in pencil and charcoal portraits. Jane was crowned Miss Africanada 2000-2001. Jane currently lives with her husband in Toronto.

nah-ee-lah/naila belvett

Naila writes, works and lives in English, French and Jamaican patois. nah-ee-lah's writing manifests into poetry, theatre, music, articles & film. She has performed in Canada, the United States and South Africa. Her debut spoken word album *nah-ee-lah:free dome* won the 2002 UMAC award for best spoken word recording. Her plays include *yagayah*, co-written with d'bi.young and *stuck*. nah-ee-lah is currently working on a second album and her first short film *muted tongue*. She holds a BA with distinction in Journalism from Concordia University and is currently pursuing a joint MFA & MBA at York university. www.nah-ee-lah.com

Peculiar I

Peculiar I (Anthony Davis) was born in Kingston Jamaica. As a high school student, Peculiar I encountered the dub poetry of Mutabaruka, a poet whose words fired his imagination. This proved to be a crucial awakening for him. With spiritual grounding, revolutionary influences, the experience of ghetto life and his education as a civil engineer, the perfect mix had been achieved to facilitate the explosion that was forthcoming. Called the "crying poet" by his peers, Peculiar I's dynamic stage performance is unforgettable. His poems can be found in *ILLUSIONS OF I* (1991). His debut album *They Called Me Madness* was nominated for a Juno in 2002.

Kevin Reigh

Kevin Reigh is a Toronto based writer/performer committed to exploring the connections between what is written, what is read, what is heard and what is said. In 2001, Kevin co-founded the Tallawa Arts Project, an arts based collective that fuses the spoken word, dance and music for performance. Kevin has performed at shows throughout the Toronto area, including – Dance Immersion's in-studio presentation (2001), Harbourfront Centre' s Masala, Mehndi, Masti festival (2001) and Dance Immersion's showcase presentation at the Du Maurier Theatre Centre (2003). Kevin is currently working on his first volume of poetry to be titled *i love, universes, all things*.

Karen Richardson

(See About the Editors, pg #180)

Dwayne Sewell

Toronto-born Dwayne Sewell moved to Jamaica before his first birthday in 1975. There, he learned about his culture through stories passed down by the elders. At age twelve, Dwayne returned to Canada. Finding support in the church, Dwayne began to write about his relationship with God. He writes about finding himself in this new world and culture. Dwayne now shares the stage with Planted, a poetic trio, implementing elements of gospel, hip-hop and reggae. His work gives praise and worship to the most high God. Dwayne resides in Brampton with his children and wife Lorraine.

Adrian Small (graphic design)

Toronto-born Adrian Small (DJ 187) was raised in Barrie, Ontario and Barbados, West Indies before coming to the T.O. suburb of Brampton. In Barrie, frustration from futile attempts to be viewed as equal led him to focus that energy into his sketchpad. Living in Barbados set the foundation for a positive self image as a member of a community. Returning to Canada enabled him to hone in on his artistic abilities, completing the graphic design programs at George Brown and Humber College. The influence of hip-hop is seen in Adrian's work as a DJ and visual artist. He currently operates his own business, Tri-One (Trinity-One) Enterprise, providing graphic design services and sound production needs.

Evon Smith

Evon Smith began writing in response to painful experiences in his childhood. As he dedicated his life to serving Jesus Christ. The themes of his poetic writings address victory, servitude and joy.   He hopes that those who feel defeated will learn that victory is near.   Ultimately, Evon hopes that his poetry will be a means for God to teach, lift downcast spirits and heal souls.   Evon is very active in his community promoting wholesome events that encourage fellowship. He recently started the Christian entertainment resource www.locus3.com with fellow poet Del Miller.   Evon is a student at Tyndale College in Toronto.

Al St. Louis

Al St.Louis was introduced to poetry through the trials and triumphs of life. Al performs as a spoken word artist on many stages throughout the Toronto. He has been a poet all of his life, recording his works since 1998. Currently, Al is the founder and host of When Words Are Spoken, a platform created for artists to share their "Word" with like-minded individuals, whether seasoned or new to the art of spoken word. He performs. Believing that spoken word will be the next great medium for change, Al hopes to be there as one of its leaders.

Kwame Stephens

Performing at venues such as the Harbourfront Centre and the Toronto Street Festival in Toronto, Kwame Stephens (Edward Ulzen) has entertained audiences for over a decade. His writing examines issues affecting the modern black man. Themes in Kwame's poetry, essays and scripts span culture, family, love and sexuality. Mr. Stephens has been affiliated with numerous cultural/social groups including Art Starts, Urban Alliance on Race Relations and Caliban Arts Theatre. He has tried his hand at almost every genre of writing – fiction, non fiction, poetry, screenplays, creative writing and corporate communication.

Christine Thompson*

Christine Thompson lives in Brampton, Ontario with both of her parents, Vernal and Beryl. She has two brothers, Christopher and Gilbert, a sister, Geraldine and a foster brother, Justin Morgan. Christine attended a private university in Huntsville, AL, majoring in English and minoring in History. Christine knew that she would be a writer since the second grade. From then on she has tried to cultivate her passion for the art of writing. To date, Christine has written two plays, three skits and four litanies. Two of her poems have been published and placed on CDs.

Asha Tomlinson

Asha Tomlinson was born and raised in Toronto. She has been dancing since the age of six with eighteen years of training in tap, jazz, modern, African, Caribbean and hip-hop dance styles. She was a member of the 2002/2003 Toronto Argonauts Dance Team. Currently, she teaches hip-hop classes at Dance Fusion Studio and is the founder and Senior Artistic Director of Black Magic Dance Company. She developed a love affair with writing in high school. She completed a Bachelor of Arts degree at the University of Windsor, majoring in Communication Studies. At present, Asha works as a news writer for City TV.

Wendy Vincent

Wendy is employed by the Canadian Broadcasting Corporation as a communications officer; working as a freelance publicist, event planner and writer on the side. Clients include: Motion, CHRY FM, The Chakra Spa, Caliban Arts and Burke's Bookstore. She was previously published by Sister Vision Press and other publications in the United States. She sits on the board of directors for the Canadian Association of Black Journalists (CABJ), the Urban Music Association of Canada (UMAC) and the US based National Association of Black Female Executives in Music and Entertainment (NABFEME).

Melville A. White

Raised in the salubrious hills of Brown's Town in the parish of St. Ann, Jamaica, Melville 'Mello' White lives in exile from his roots. Presently domiciled in Toronto, Melville poignantly uses the language of poetry and local vernacular to relate a narrative of engagement, conflict and the sometimes calamitous consequences that arise from the collision of diverse worldviews. His contribution is from a soon-to-be published collection of poems entitled, *After Dark©*. His love ballads are published in *Love Rhapsodies and Blues©*. He is a partner in a new media and entertainment company, Mouth Wide Shut™. Melville currently works as a social worker.

Nana Yeboaa

Nana Yeboaa (Bernadette Poku) was born and raised in Ghana, West Africa. She is a graduate of the University of Toronto with a honours BA in Health Studies and Sociology and a minor in Anthropology. She has been writing since the age of 15. She has been published in the Marginalia, Unique Magazine and the coming APUS students *Coming to Voice* anthology. Her work focuses on the depiction of family and community images and themes in a traditional Ghanian context. Nana is presently working of a collection of poems for publication.

About The Editors

Steven Green*

Born in Branson Hospital, Toronto to Jamaican parents, Steven Green was raised in Scarborough before moving to Orlando, Florida at age fourteen. Holding a Bachelor's degree in African and Caribbean History from the University of Florida, his poetry and prose is informed by said history. His written work explores the intersection of cultures, ideals and emotions.

He moved to Boston in 2000 to become a teacher at Boston High School. Teaching in the Boston public school system heightened Steven's awareness of the skills necessary to inspire learning in black youth.

Steven works in theatre, primarily as a production manager. Credits include, *da kink in my hair* (Plaitform Entertainment), *rock.paper.sistahz* (b current), *3 parts harmony* (b current), *The Piano Lesson* (Obsidian) and *The Adventures of a Black Girl in Search of God* (Mirvish). In 2001, he was commissioned to write T*he Real McCoy* for Markham Gateway Public School. T-*Dot Griots: An Anthology of Toronto's Black Storytellers* is Steven Green's first title as editor.

Karen Richardson

Karen Richardson is a performance poet, event producer and journalist. She has delivered her words on stage since 1995, having entertained thousands in Toronto, Halifax, Ottawa, Montreal and New York. Her words are poignant. Her voice is powerful. Citing Austin Clarke, Fred Hammond, Guru of Gangstarr and Toni Morrison as her influences, Karen believes "art is organic and creativity is innate in all of humanity. It is our most obvious connection to our creator." As the founder of Mustard Seed Productions, she is driven to increase dialogue among African Canadians. Recognizing an individual's sphere of influence is potentially universal; Karen hopes to reach the world with her message of reconciliation to God.

She is the organizer and host of the interactive La Parole arts series: Toronto's Speech Therapy for the Creative Mind. She has produced arts showcases in both Toronto and Montreal, beginning in 1998. Such events as Polyphony, Freedom Jam, Mustard Seed, Planted, La Parole and Idiom collectively have featured the works of over one hundred Canadian artists; be they actors, comedians, poets, dancers, fashion designers, emcees, instrumentalists, playwrights, singers, storytellers or visual artists.

As a writer she has contributed articles to publications including: Cantos Cadre, Unique, The McGill Daily and N'jozi (Buffalo, New York). Karen holds a BA in Political Science and Economics from McGill University, where she was the Political Coordinator of the Black Students Network and an on-air contributor to Soul Perspectives (CKUT 90.3 FM).

Born in Scarborough, Ontario, Karen Richardson was raised and currently lives in Brampton. She attends Bramalea Baptist Church where she sits on the design team as coordinator of the poetic arts ministry. She is currently completing a novel and a book of her poetic works. Karen will record an album of her original songs and poems with Hysyanz Records, St. Vincent, West Indies in 2004.

*Photos taken by Davidson Elie

ISBN 155395631-1

9 781553 956310